Breads

GENERAL EDITOR
CHUCK WILLIAMS

RECIPES
JACQUELINE MALLORCA

PHOTOGRAPHY
ALLAN ROSENBERG

TIME
LIFE
BOOKS

TIME-LIFE BOOKS
Time-Life Books is a division of Time Life Inc.
Time-Life is a trademark of Time Warner Inc. U.S.A.

A Note on Weights and Measures:
All recipes include customary U.S. and metric measurements. Metric conversions are based on a standard developed for these books and have been rounded off. Actual weights may vary.

Time-Life Custom Publishing
Vice President and Publisher: Terry Newell
Director of New Product Development: Regina Hall
Managing Editor: Donia Ann Steele
Director of Sales: Neil Levin
Director of Financial Operations: J. Brian Birky

WILLIAMS-SONOMA
Founder/Vice-Chairman: Chuck Williams

WELDON OWEN INC.
President: John Owen
Vice President and Publisher: Wendely Harvey
Vice President and CFO: Richard VanOosterhout
Associate Publisher: Laurie Wertz
Managing Editor: Lisa Chaney Atwood
Consulting Editor: Norman Kolpas
Copy Editor: Sharon Silva
Design: John Bull, The Book Design Company
Production Director: Stephanie Sherman
Production Coordinator: Tarji Mickelson
Production Editor: Janique Gascoigne
Co-Editions Director: Derek Barton
Food Photographer: Allan Rosenberg
Additional Food Photography: Allen V. Lott
Primary Food Stylist: Heidi Gintner
Primary Prop Stylist: Sandra Griswold
Assistant Food Stylists: Nette Scott, Elizabeth C. Davis,
    Jeffrey Lord
Assistant Prop Stylist: Elizabeth C. Davis
Glossary Illustrations: Alice Harth

The Williams-Sonoma Kitchen Library
conceived and produced by Weldon Owen Inc.
814 Montgomery St., San Francisco, CA 94133

In collaboration with Williams-Sonoma
3250 Van Ness Ave., San Francisco, CA 94109

Production by Mandarin Offset, Hong Kong
Printed in China

A Weldon Owen Production

Copyright © 1996 Weldon Owen Inc.
Reprinted in 1996

Library of Congress
Cataloging-in-Publication Data:

Mallorca, Jacqueline.
    Breads / general editor, Chuck Williams :
    recipes, Jacqueline Mallorca ; photography, Allan Rosenberg.
        p.   cm. — (Williams-Sonoma kitchen library)
    ISBN 0-7835-0316-4
    1. Breads.   I. Williams, Chuck.   II. Title.   III. Series.
TX769.M324   1996
641.8'15—dc20   95-47664
                                         CIP

Contents

INTRODUCTION

"Man cannot live by bread alone," goes the familiar old saw. To which I'd like to add my own elaboration: "Neither can he dine well without it."

Bread makes a good meal great. What, after all, is a sandwich without slices cut from a fresh, crusty loaf? What is a stew or a pasta sauce without a hunk of bread to sop up every last drop? What is a morning meal without golden toast or a sweet breakfast bun?

But why bother to make your own bread when so many fine bakeries exist today? This book goes a long way toward answering that question. It shows you, first of all, how easy it is to make bread with reliable commercial yeasts and flours that yield consistently good results and provides simplified step-by-step instructions that reduce even the most involved recipes to a few essentials. These basics are followed by 44 recipes for familiar, favorite loaves, as well as wonderful breads you're not likely to find in any store—from Italian focaccia and pizza to a Scandinavian beer bread, Portuguese corn bread and Swedish cardamom twist. With a few pieces of special equipment, a handful of basic ingredients and a little practice, your efforts will surpass even those of the best local bakeries.

Let me add here a personal observation on making bread. Although yeast loaves do take several hours from start to finish, most of that time is occupied in the dough rising; your work involves just minutes of easily mastered techniques. I've always found that bread making works best as an afternoon and evening activity on a leisurely weekend, when you have other things to do around the house. And the biggest payoff for the time you invest is the wonderful aroma that fills your kitchen, drawing everyone else in the house so irresistibly that you really could swear we *do* live by bread alone.

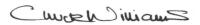

EQUIPMENT

Most bread making can be carried out with only the most basic kitchen tools

For the most part, bread baking requires only everyday cooking equipment—a bowl, a spoon and a baking sheet are all that is needed. But as you find yourself becoming more interested in making a greater variety of breads, you may want to invest in a stand mixer and an array of baking pans and tools to broaden your bread-making repertoire.

1. Electric Stand Mixer
Heavy-duty countertop mixer with stainless-steel bowl, and dough hook attachment for kneading.

2. Baking Pan
Shallow metal pan to hold water on the oven floor to produce steam during baking, promoting crisper crusts.

3. Assorted Utensils
Crockery jar holds wooden spoons for stirring bread batters and doughs (their round handles also assist in forming the holes in the centers of bagels), and rubber spatulas for scraping down the sides of bowls in which batters are prepared and for smoothing the surface of batters before baking.

4. Baguette Pan
Baking pan composed of half-cylindrical 18-by-6-inch (45-by-15-cm) molds for forming and baking the classic elongated French loaves known as baguettes.

5. Baking Sheet with Rim
Metal 11-by-17-inch (28-by-43-cm) baking sheet with 1-inch (2.5-cm) sides for baking focaccia and other flat breads. Choose heavy metal sheets that will conduct heat evenly and will not buckle.

6. Liquid Measuring Cup
For accurate measuring of liquid ingredients. Choose heavy-duty heat-resistant glass with measurements in cups, ounces and milliliters.

7. Spray Bottle
All-purpose pump-action spray bottle, available in houseware stores and beauty supply shops, for spritzing the sides and floor of an oven during baking to create steam for crisp crusts.

8. Cutting Board
Large wooden board provides a flat work surface for kneading and shaping bread doughs.

9. Dry Measuring Cups
In graduated sizes, for accurate measuring of dry ingredients. Straight rims allow ingredients to be leveled for accuracy. Choose stainless steel for sturdiness.

10. Measuring Spoons
In graduated sizes, for measuring small quantities of ingredients such as yeast, baking powder and salt. Select good-quality, calibrated metal spoons with deep bowls.

11. Pastry Scraper
Assists in the early stages of kneading very soft doughs by hand, making lifting them easier. Also useful for scraping work surfaces clean during and after kneading.

12. Wire Racks
Sturdy stainless-steel racks hold breads of all shapes and sizes, allowing air to circulate under them for quick, even cooling after baking.

13. Muffin Rings
Traditional metal rings measuring 3½ inches (9 cm) in diameter, for forming English muffins.

14. Sharp Knife
Small, sharp knife for slashing the tops of bread loaves. A single-edged razor blade may also be used.

15. Bread Knife
The ideal knife for slicing bread, with a long, straight, sharp serrated blade well attached to a sturdy handle.

16. Kitchen Scissors
Useful for cutting bread dough into smaller pieces, and particularly for the fine cutting necessary when shaping an elaborate loaf such as a wheat sheaf or a twist.

17. Rolling Pin
Choose a rolling pin with ball-bearing handles for smooth rolling, and a hardwood surface at least 12 inches (30 cm) long. To prevent warping, do not wash; wipe clean with a damp cloth.

18. Baking Sheet
Heavy-duty rimless metal sheet pan for holding free-form loaves and rolls.

19. Pizza Pan
Circular pan with perforated surface to promote circulation of heat for quicker-baking, crisper pizza crusts.

20. Bread Pans
The 8-inch (20-cm) square cake pan is used for making sticky buns and other break fast breads; the 8½-by-4½-inch (21.5-by-11.5-cm) pan yields a standard rectangular loaf; and the 8-inch (20-cm) round cake pan may be used to hold and shape some round loaves. Note that most recipes require at least 2 pans of the same size to bake their full yield.

21. Kitchen Towels
For covering bread doughs during rising and for wrapping just-baked loaves to capture moisture and help promote soft crusts. Choose good-quality, sturdy cotton towels.

22. Glass Mixing Bowls
Bowls in graduated sizes for all-purpose kitchen use. Their nonporous surfaces will not react with bread ingredients.

23. Food Processor
Quickly mixes simple doughs, pulverizes grains to fine meal, and aids in the chopping or puréeing of ingredients. Choose a model with a powerful motor; it is less likely to stall when mixing stiff doughs.

24. Charlotte Mold
Traditional French bucket-shaped, tinned-steel mold, ideal for baking cylindrical loaves such as batter breads.

25. Large Mixing Bowls
Sturdy, deep, large-capacity bowls for mixing bread doughs by hand and for holding doughs while they rise. Heavy earthenware bowls are non-reactive and retain heat, helping to promote rising.

26. Brioche Mold
Traditional fluted, tinned-steel mold for baking the classic egg- and butter-enriched French loaves and other, similarly rich breads.

27. Porcelain Soufflé Dish
Classic 1-qt (1-l) dish may be used for baking batter breads and other cylindrical loaves.

28. Pastry Brushes
Large and small brushes for applying glazes to breads. Choose sturdy wooden-handled brushes with well-attached bristles.

29. Citrus Reamer
Old-fashioned wooden device for extracting the juice from halved lemons and other citrus fruits.

30. Metal Spatula
Wide, square-cornered spatula efficiently moves small breads or rolls to and from baking sheets and pans.

Bread Baking Basics

A simple guide to flours, leavenings, liquids, fats and flavorings—the basic ingredients that form the foundation of all home-baked breads

At its most basic, good bread is made from flour, yeast and water. Understanding the properties of these basic ingredients will make your bread making all the more pleasurable, and lead you to a wide range of variations.

Flour. Wheat contains a protein known as gluten that, when combined with water, becomes elastic. When dough is kneaded, gluten forms a web that traps the gas released by yeast, causing bread to rise and develop a fine, honeycombed "crumb," or texture.

Different wheat varieties have varying gluten contents. "Hard" wheat, the source of bread flour, has the most, 12.5 percent, while all-purpose (plain) flour, a blend of hard and lower-gluten "soft" wheats, has only 9 percent. Because of its higher gluten content, bread flour will rise higher and produce a more airy-textured loaf.

This book calls for *unbleached* bread flour. Bleaching, the chemical process used to whiten flour, inhibits gluten. Unbleached flour is whitened through an aging process that does not affect gluten.

Leavening. When combined with flour and liquid, yeast feeds on the flour's starch and releases gas that raises bread. The most common forms of yeast available today are active dry yeast, ideal for breads that gain flavor and texture from slower rising; and quick-rise yeast, which raises breads in as little as half the time of active dry yeast, making simple loaves all the more convenient. Neither of these commercial yeasts requires the old-fashioned "proofing" step still found in some cookbooks, as long as it is used before the package expiration date.

Some breads in this book are also leavened by baking soda, which releases carbon dioxide gas to raise doughs or batters quickly.

Liquids. Most breads are made with water, but other liquids can contribute richness and flavor. Milk yields soft, delicate bread. Buttermilk adds tang, and beer, heartiness. Any liquid should be warmed to about 110°F (43°C) to promote the yeast's activity. Liquid that is too hot will kill the yeast, while liquid that is too cool will slow the dough's leavening. Use an instant-read thermometer to accurately measure the temperature of liquid. Once you become accustomed to bread making, gauging temperature may be accomplished simply by touch.

Fats. Butter, oil and other fats make bread richer and more tender, as well as contribute flavor.

Flavorings. Salt strengthens gluten, controls yeast and enhances the flavor of other ingredients. Sugar not only sweetens dough but increases yeast's activity and caramelizes for a browner crust. All kinds of other flavorings—from cocoa to nuts, herbs to spices—can contribute still more distinction to individual bread doughs.

FLOURS AND GRAINS

While most breads are made from some form of wheat flour alone, many other grains provide flours that, when used in combination with wheat flour, yield breads with richly varied flavors, textures and colors.

All-Purpose (Plain) Flour
Blend of high- and low-gluten flours. May replace bread flour, with slightly denser, more cakelike results.

Unbleached Bread Flour
Flour ground from the endosperm of hard wheat, yielding a high-gluten product ideal for bread.

Whole-Wheat (Wholemeal) Flour
Ground from the whole wheat kernel. Richer in flavor and texture, but does not rise as easily as white flours.

Rye Flour
Provides rich, sour flavor. Low in gluten, it yields a dense texture and is usually combined with wheat flour.

Brown-Rice Flour
Fine, nutty-tasting flour ground from whole rice grains. Available in natural-foods stores or by mail.

Chestnut Flour
Sweet, starchy flour ground from chestnuts. Available in Italian delicatessens and natural food stores.

Gluten Flour
Made from hard wheat that has been milled to intensify its protein and thus its gluten; generally used in combination with low-gluten flours.

Polenta
White or yellow Italian cornmeal with a coarse, even grind. Use long-cooking polenta imported from Italy.

Corn Flour
Finely ground yellow corn-meal. Available in natural-foods stores or by mail order.

Rolled Oats
Rich, nutty flakes of oat flattened by heated rollers after cleaning and hulling. Widely available.

Bran
The outer coating of whole grains such as wheat and oats. Provides rich flavor, texture and fiber.

MAKING YEAST BREADS

A few easy steps provide simple strategies for making yeast bread

At first glance, making yeast-leavened bread might seem like a lot of work, and there are, as you can see from the basic demonstration at right, many steps to its preparation. But when you analyze the process further, you'll discover that the actual hands-on work takes no more than about 20 minutes of your time, with the remaining 3 hours or so consumed by the bread rising or baking on its own.

In the first stage of making yeast bread, the dough is prepared. This demonstration begins with dissolving the yeast. You'll find that many of the recipes in this book take advantage of the reliability and speed of quick-rise yeast by combining it directly with other dry ingredients. In either case, liquids should be at about 110°F (43°C), the optimum temperature for activating yeast.

Some people prefer to mix dough by hand (step 2a), but an electric stand mixer fitted with the paddle attachment can do the job more easily (2b). Plus, when the mixer is fitted with the dough hook, it can also assist in the kneading that develops the dough's web of gluten (3b).

Two risings—one after kneading, another after shaping—further develop the dough's lightness and texture. Dough rises best in a warm, draft-free environment. For convenience, most doughs can be allowed to rise more slowly by placing them in the refrigerator overnight.

Always bake bread on the oven's middle rack. Many of the recipes in this book yield more than one loaf of bread. Because home-baked breads lack the preservatives found in commercial loaves, any extras should be wrapped airtight and stored in the freezer, where they will keep for up to 3 months.

1. Dissolving the yeast.
In a mixing bowl, dissolve the yeast in lukewarm (110°F/43°C) liquid—here, water. Let stand for about 5 minutes, at which point the yeast will begin to bubble slightly.

2a. Mixing by hand.
Add seasonings and about two-thirds of the flour, stirring with a sturdy wooden spoon. Gradually stir in just enough of the remaining flour to form a dough with the consistency described in the recipe.

5. Letting the dough rise.
Cover the bowl loosely with plastic wrap and leave it at warm room temperature to rise as directed, most often until doubled in bulk.

6. Pressing out air bubbles.
Turn out the risen dough onto a lightly floured work surface. Using both hands, press out any remaining pockets of air to promote an even texture in the finished loaf.

2b. Mixing in an electric mixer.
Alternatively, combine the yeast mixture with seasonings and about two-thirds of the flour in the bowl of an electric stand mixer with the paddle attachment set on low speed. Gradually add more flour to form the desired dough consistency.

3a. Kneading by hand.
Turn out the dough onto a lightly floured work surface. Knead by folding the dough over, then pressing down and away with the heel of your hand. Give the dough a quarter turn and repeat, adding flour as necessary to avoid stickiness, until smooth and elastic.

3b. Kneading by dough hook.
Alternatively, replace the mixer's paddle with a dough hook attachment and knead on medium speed until the dough is no longer sticky and pulls away from the sides of the bowl.

4. Placing the dough in a greased bowl.
Lightly grease a large glass or glazed earthenware bowl, using whatever fat was used in the dough or flavorless vegetable oil. Put the dough in the bowl and turn it to coat all sides lightly.

7. Letting the shaped loaf rise.
Shape the dough, following instructions in the individual recipe. Place on a greased baking sheet or in a pan, cover loosely with greased plastic wrap or a kitchen towel and leave at warm room temperature to rise as directed.

8. Glazing the loaf.
While the loaf rises, preheat the oven to the specified baking temperature. Just before baking, uncover the loaf and brush gently with whatever glaze is called for in the recipe.

9. Slashing the loaf.
To provide a controlled, decorative place from which the loaf can release gas during baking, many loaves are slashed on the surface. Use a small, sharp knife or a single-edged razor blade, cutting in decisive strokes usually about ½ inch (12 mm) deep.

10. Checking doneness.
Put the loaf on the oven's middle rack and bake for the specified time—creating steam with a spray bottle or pan of water, if the recipe requires—until the loaf has darkened to the color indicated and sounds hollow when its bottom is tapped.

Shaping Techniques

Easy steps for shaping bread dough, from simple rounds and sandwich loaves to elaborate presentations for a holiday table

Round Loaves

The most basic of bread shapes, the round loaf nonetheless requires some technique to ensure an even, well-risen form.

Stretching the sides down.
After pressing the risen dough flat, form it into a ball. With both hands, stretch the sides of the dough downward and under, rotating the ball as you do so to form a tight, compact shape. Pinch the seam closed to seal.

Braided Loaves

Braiding, the traditional form for an egg braid (page 24), is one of the easiest ways to prepare bread dough for a festive presentation.

Braiding dough.
Start with 3 ropes of dough of the length specified and pinch them together at one end. Braid them by alternately twisting the left- and right-hand ropes over the center. Pinch the ends to seal.

Rectangular Loaves

All kinds of basic doughs may be baked in a loaf pan. Rolling up the dough and pinching its seams closed ensures a uniform, well-risen shape and even texture for the finished loaf.

1. Rolling up the dough.
With a rolling pin, roll out a ball of dough into a flat, even rectangle of size specified. Starting at a short side, roll up the rectangle like a jelly roll.

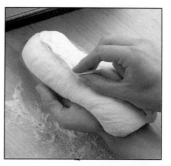

2. Pinching the seams closed.
With your fingertips, pinch together the long seam and the spiral seams on both ends to seal them. Place the dough in a greased loaf pan with its long seam down.

TWISTED LOAVES

Rolling and snipping dough results in an enticing presentation for a Swedish cardamom twist (page 91). The same technique may be used to make a circular loaf, baked in a round pan.

HARVEST WHEAT SHEAF

Following the recipe on page 102, divide the dough into three balls and use the first ball to form the sheaf base. Follow the steps below to complete this elaborate edible centerpiece.

1. Cutting the rolled dough.
Spread a rectangle of dough with a filling and roll it up jelly-roll style as for a loaf pan loaf (opposite). Transfer, seam side down, to a pre-pared baking sheet. Using scissors and cutting at an angle, snip the roll at ½-inch (12-mm) intervals, cutting almost halfway through.

1. Placing the "stalks."
Cut the second ball of dough in half. Set aside one-half to use for the "tie" and roll out the other half into a rectangle ¼ inch (6 mm) thick. Cut into thin strands and roll them into thin ropes. Brush the lower third of the sheaf's prepared dough base with egg glaze and arrange the dough strands on top like stalks of wheat.

2. Twisting the cut dough.
With the fingers of both hands, pull and push the snipped sections of dough alternately to the left and right, twisting each section slightly in the process to expose the spiral inside.

2. Cutting the "ears."
Roll out the third ball of dough about ¼ inch (6 mm) thick and cut out 1-inch (2.5-cm) diamonds. With a small knife, make two cuts on each of two adjacent edges to resemble ears of wheat. Brush the upper section of the base with egg glaze and arrange the ears in rows starting at the top, overlapping the edges of the base slightly.

3. "Tying" the sheaf.
Cut the reserved ball of dough into 3 equal pieces. Roll each piece into a rope about 10 inches (25 cm) long and braid tightly as for a braided loaf (opposite). Place the braid across the stalks at the narrowest part of the base. Tuck the ends underneath the base to secure.

Candied Citrus Peel

Unlike most commercial varieties, homemade candied citrus peel contains all the natural aromatic oils of the fruit's peel, making it particularly flavorful. Although the cooking process is spread over several days, it is not difficult and the results are spectacular. A popular addition to holiday breads, these semitransparent glacéed citrus peels also make a wonderful holiday gift. You can store them in lock-top plastic bags in the refrigerator for up to 1 month or in the freezer for up to 6 months. If possible, buy organically grown fruits with thin skins.

8 large lemons or 6 medium oranges (*see note*)
3 qt (3 l) water
1 tablespoon salt
3¼ cups (26 oz/810 g) sugar

Using a stiff-bristled brush, scrub the fruits under running water. Cut crosswise into halves. Using a citrus reamer, extract all the juice and reserve for another purpose. Pull out the membranes, which come away easily, leaving just the colored outer shells and white pith.

In a large bowl, combine the water and salt and stir to dissolve the salt. Add the citrus peels and let soak for 1 hour to draw out the bitterness from the pith. Drain and rinse well.

In a saucepan over high heat, combine the peels with water to cover. Bring to a boil, then reduce the heat to low and simmer until tender when pierced with the tip of a knife, about 1 hour. Remove from the heat and drain well, reserving the cooking liquid.

Measure the cooking liquid and add enough water to total 4 cups (32 fl oz/1 l). Place in a nonaluminum saucepan and add 2 cups (1 lb/500 g) sugar. Bring to a boil over high heat, stirring to dissolve the sugar, and boil for 5 minutes. Add the peels, reduce the heat to low and simmer for 5 minutes. Remove from the heat and transfer the peels and syrup to a bowl. Cover and refrigerate for 2 days.

Drain off the syrup into a nonaluminum saucepan. Add 1 cup (8 oz/250 g) sugar and bring to a boil. Add the peels, reduce the heat to low and simmer until semitransparent, about 40 minutes.

Remove from the heat, pour the peels and syrup into a bowl and let cool. Cover and let stand at room temperature for 4–6 hours.

Drain off the syrup, measure it and add enough water to total 2 cups (16 fl oz/500 ml). Place in a nonaluminum saucepan and add ¼ cup (2 oz/60 g) sugar. Bring to a boil over high heat, add the peels and boil for 5 minutes.

Using a slotted spoon, remove the peels from the syrup and place, colored sides up, on a wire rack set over a large plate to catch drips. Let dry at room temperature for 12 hours. Chop just before using.

Makes about 1 lb (500 g)

Tapenade

This Mediterranean mixture is a delicious spread and imparts a wonderful tang to rustic French and Italian breads. If you plan to store it for more than a few days, pour a thin layer of olive oil over the top to seal out the air, then cover and refrigerate for up to 2 months.

½ lb (250 g) oil-cured black olives, pitted
2 tablespoons olive oil
2 cloves garlic, chopped
1 tablespoon well-drained capers
½ teaspoon herbes de Provence
freshly ground pepper

*I*n a food processor fitted with the metal blade or in a blender, combine the olives, olive oil, garlic, capers, herbs and pepper to taste. Pulse until the mixture is evenly chopped. Transfer to a container with a tight-fitting lid and store in the refrigerator (see note).

*Makes about ¾ cup
(4½ oz/140 g)*

Sourdough Starter

A reliable method for initiating the fermentation process needed to develop a good sourdough starter is to use commercial yeast in a flour-and-water mixture. Properly prepared, the mixture should bubble up and develop a good sour aroma. If your starter develops a foul odor or a pinkish color, it has gone bad and should be promptly thrown away.

1 package (2¼ teaspoons) active dry yeast
2½ cups (20 fl oz/625 ml) lukewarm water
    (110°F/43°C), plus lukewarm water as
    needed for feeding starter
2½ cups (12½ oz/390 g) unbleached bread flour,
    plus flour as needed for feeding starter

*I*n a glass or earthenware bowl, combine the yeast and ½ cup (4 fl oz/125 ml) of the lukewarm water and let stand until bubbles start to rise, about 5 minutes. Stir in the 2½ cups (12½ oz/390 g) flour and the remaining 2 cups (16 fl oz/500 ml) lukewarm water and mix well. Pour into a 4-qt (4-l) or larger ceramic or glass crock and cover with cheesecloth (muslin). Let stand for 4 days in a warm place (70–75°F/21–24°C). The mixture will bubble and ferment, increasing 4–6 times in volume and then sinking to its original size.

Transfer the starter to a tightly covered glass container and store in the refrigerator. Feed the starter every 10 days by stirring in ½ cup (2½ oz/75 g) flour and ½ cup (4 fl oz/125 ml) lukewarm water. Each time the starter is used, reserve at least 1 cup (8 fl oz/250 ml) of the original mixture and replace the amount taken with equal amounts of flour and lukewarm water. Bring to room temperature and stir gently before using.

Makes about 4 cups (32 fl oz/1 l)

Old-Fashioned White Bread

5–6 cups (25–30 oz/780–940 g)
  unbleached bread flour
2 teaspoons salt
1 package (2¼ teaspoons) quick-rise
  yeast
1 cup (8 fl oz/250 ml) water
1 cup (8 fl oz/250 ml) milk
3 tablespoons unsalted butter
1 egg yolk beaten with 1 teaspoon
  water, for glaze *Do not*
        Use – it browns
        too fast

This is a genuine home-style white loaf with excellent flavor and texture. Use it for sandwiches, toast, croutons or bread crumbs.

*I*n a large bowl or the bowl of an electric stand mixer, combine 4 cups (1¼ lb/625 g) of the flour, the salt and yeast. In a saucepan over low heat, combine the water, milk and butter. Heat briefly, stirring often, until lukewarm (110°F/43°C). Gradually stir the water mixture into the flour mixture, adding enough of the remaining flour to make a soft dough that holds its shape.

Knead by hand or with a dough hook, adding flour as necessary. Knead by hand until smooth and elastic, about 10 minutes; knead by hook until dough is not sticky and pulls cleanly from the bowl sides, 6–7 minutes. (See directions on pages 10–11.)

Form the dough into a ball and place in a clean, greased bowl, turning to grease all sides. Cover with plastic wrap and let rise until doubled, 45–60 minutes.

Grease two 8½-by-4½-inch (21.5-by-11.5-cm) loaf pans. Turn out the dough onto a lightly floured work surface and press flat. Cut in half and form each half into a ball. Using a rolling pin, roll out each ball into a 12-by-7-inch (30-by-18-cm) rectangle. Starting from a short side, roll up the dough like a jelly roll. Pinch the seams and ends to seal and place in the prepared pans, seam sides down. Cover loosely with greased plastic wrap; let rise in a warm place until doubled, 30–45 minutes. Preheat an oven to 400°F (200°C).

Brush the loaves with the glaze. Bake until golden brown and the loaves sound hollow when tapped on the bottoms, 30–40 minutes. Unmold the loaves and transfer to a wire rack to cool.

Makes two 1¼-lb (625-g) loaves

French Baguettes

5–5½ cups (25–27½ oz/780–855 g)
   unbleached bread flour
2 teaspoons salt
1 package (2¼ teaspoons) quick-rise
   yeast
2 cups (16 fl oz/500 ml) lukewarm
   water (110°F/43°C)
boiling water, as needed
cornmeal for pans
1 egg white beaten with pinch of salt,
   for glaze

*If you do not have a mixer, lift and turn the dough with a pastry
scraper until it develops enough body to knead by hand.*

⚜

*I*n the bowl of an electric stand mixer, combine 4 cups (1¼ lb/
625 g) of the flour, the salt, yeast and water. Stir until blended.
Knead with the dough hook until the dough is elastic and pulls
cleanly from the bowl sides, about 10 minutes, adding flour as
needed. The dough will be very soft. Turn out onto a lightly
floured surface and knead for 1 minute. Form into a ball and
place in a clean bowl. Dust lightly with flour, cover with plastic
wrap and let rise in a warm place until doubled, 45–60 minutes.

   Scrape the dough out onto a well-floured work surface. Press
flat, knead for a few seconds and return to the bowl. Cover with
plastic wrap and let rise again until doubled, 20–30 minutes.

   Line each of 2 double baguette pans (4 molds total), each 18
inches (45 cm) long and 6 inches (15 cm) wide, with a kitchen
towel and sprinkle with flour, lightly rubbing it into the fabric.
Turn out the dough onto a floured work surface; press flat. Cut
into 4 equal pieces, knead into balls and let rest for 5 minutes.
Press each ball flat and then fold into thirds. Roll each into a rope
16 inches (40 cm) long with tapered ends. Place in the towel-
lined pans. Cover with a kitchen towel and let rise until doubled,
about 20 minutes. Preheat an oven to 450°F (230°C).

   Place a shallow pan of boiling water on the floor of the preheated oven. Pull the pans out from under the towels. Grease
the pans and sprinkle with cornmeal. One at a time, flip the
loaves into the pans, underside up. Brush with the glaze. Using
a sharp knife, make three ¼-inch (6-mm) deep diagonal slashes
on each loaf. Bake until brown and crusty, 20–25 minutes. Transfer the loaves to a wire rack. Serve warm or at room temperature.

Makes four ½-lb (250-g) baguettes

Buttermilk Bread

1 package (2¼ teaspoons) active dry
  yeast
1 cup (8 fl oz/250 ml) lukewarm water
  (110°F/43°C)
5½–6 cups (27½–30 oz/855–940 g)
  unbleached bread flour
2 teaspoons sugar
2 teaspoons salt
¼ teaspoon baking soda (bicarbonate
  of soda)
1 cup (8 fl oz/250 ml) buttermilk
6 tablespoons (3 oz/90 g) unsalted
  butter

This old-fashioned bread has a pleasant, tender crumb.

*I*n a small bowl, dissolve the yeast in the lukewarm water and let stand until bubbles start to rise, about 5 minutes. In a large bowl, mix together 2 cups (10 oz/315 g) of the flour, the sugar, salt and baking soda.

In a saucepan over low heat, combine the buttermilk and butter. Heat briefly, stirring often, until lukewarm (110°F/43°C). Stir the buttermilk mixture into the flour mixture. Add the yeast mixture and stir until smooth. Beat in 1 cup (5 oz/155 g) more flour to make a thick batter. Gradually stir in enough of the remaining flour to make a soft dough that holds its shape.

Knead by hand or with a dough hook, adding flour as necessary. Knead by hand until smooth and elastic, about 10 minutes; knead by hook until dough is not sticky and pulls cleanly from the bowl sides, 5–6 minutes. (See directions on pages 10–11.)

Form the dough into a ball and place in a clean, greased bowl, turning to grease all sides. Cover with plastic wrap and let rise in a warm place until doubled, 1–1½ hours.

Butter two 8½-by-4½-inch (21.5-by-11.5-cm) loaf pans. Turn out the dough onto a lightly floured work surface and press flat. Cut the dough in half. Using a rolling pin, roll out each half into a 12-by-7-inch (30-by-18-cm) rectangle. Starting from a short side, roll up like a jelly roll. Pinch the seams and ends to seal and place in the prepared pans, seam sides down. Cover loosely with greased plastic wrap and let rise until doubled, 1¼–1¾ hours.

Preheat an oven to 375°F (190°C). Uncover and bake until the loaves are golden and sound hollow when tapped on the bottoms, 35–40 minutes. Transfer the loaves to a wire rack to cool.

Makes two 22-oz (685-g) loaves

good –
take a long time to raise # San Francisco Sourdough Bread

1 package (2¼ teaspoons) active dry
  yeast
1 cup (8 fl oz/250 ml) lukewarm water
  (110°F/43°C)
2 cups (16 fl oz/500 ml) sourdough
  starter *(recipe on page 15)*, at room
  temperature
2 teaspoons salt
4–4½ cups (20–22½ oz/625–700 g)
  unbleached bread flour
cornmeal for pan

Makes 2 Small round
loaves

This dough must rise slowly in order to develop its characteristic porous crumb, crisp crust and wonderful sour tang.

❧

*I*n a large bowl or the bowl of an electric stand mixer, dissolve the yeast in the lukewarm water and let stand until bubbles start to rise, about 5 minutes. Stir in the sourdough starter, salt and 2½ cups (12½ oz/390 g) of the flour. Gradually stir in enough of the remaining flour to make a soft dough that holds its shape.

Knead by hand or with a dough hook, adding flour as necessary. Knead by hand until smooth and elastic, about 10 minutes; knead by hook until dough is not sticky and pulls cleanly from the bowl sides, 5–6 minutes. (See directions on pages 10–11.)

Form the dough into a ball and place in a clean, greased bowl, turning to grease all sides. Cover with plastic wrap and let rise in a warm place until tripled, 2–3 hours.

Dust a baking sheet with cornmeal. Turn out the dough onto a lightly floured work surface and press flat. Knead twice and cut in half. Form each half into a ball, stretching the sides down and under. Flatten each ball into a round loaf 8 inches (20 cm) in diameter. Place on the prepared sheet, cover with a kitchen towel and let rise until doubled, about 1 hour.

Preheat an oven to 450°F (230°C).

Place a shallow pan of boiling water on the floor of the preheated oven. Uncover the loaves and, using a sharp knife, slash a diagonal grid pattern on top of each one. Bake for 15 minutes, then reduce the heat to 350°F (180°C) and bake until well browned and the loaves sound hollow when tapped on the bottoms, 20–25 minutes longer. Transfer the loaves to a wire rack to cool.

Makes two 1-lb (500-g) loaves

Egg Braid

6–6½ cups (30–32 oz/940 g–1 kg)
   unbleached bread flour
2 teaspoons salt
1 package (2¼ teaspoons) quick-rise
   yeast
1 cup (8 fl oz/250 ml) water
large pinch of saffron threads
¼ cup (2 oz/60 g) unsalted butter
4 eggs, at room temperature
1 egg yolk beaten with 1 teaspoon
   water, for glaze
2 teaspoons poppyseeds

This thick, double-braided loaf is rich with eggs and saffron.

*In a large bowl or the bowl of an electric stand mixer, combine 4 cups (1¼ lb/625 g) of the flour, the salt and yeast. In a pan over low heat, combine the water, saffron and butter. Heat to warm (125°F/52°C). Stir the water mixture into the flour mixture, then beat in the eggs. Gradually stir in enough of the remaining flour to make a soft dough that holds its shape.

Knead by hand or with a dough hook, adding flour as necessary. Knead by hand until smooth and elastic, about 10 minutes; knead by hook until dough is not sticky and pulls cleanly from the bowl sides, 6–7 minutes. (See directions on pages 10–11.)

Form the dough into a ball and place in a clean, greased bowl, turning to grease all sides. Cover with plastic wrap and let rise in a warm place until doubled, 45–60 minutes.

Turn out the dough onto a lightly floured work surface and press flat. Cut in half and form each half into a ball. Let rest for 5 minutes. Roll each ball into a log 9 inches (23 cm) long and 2¼ inches (5.5 cm) in diameter. Cut one-third off the end of each log. Cut the larger section of 1 log into 3 equal pieces, then roll each piece into a rope 12 inches (30 cm) long. Braid the ropes as directed on page 12. Repeat with the smaller section to make a thinner braid. Set the small braid on top of the large one. Repeat to form a second loaf. Place the loaves on a baking sheet. Cover with greased plastic wrap and let rise until doubled, 30–45 minutes. Preheat an oven to 400°F (200°C).

Uncover the loaves, brush with the glaze and sprinkle with the poppyseeds. Bake until well browned and the loaves sound hollow when tapped on the bottoms, 35–45 minutes. Transfer the loaves to a wire rack to cool.

Makes two 18-oz (560-g) loaves

Rustic Country Loaf

2¾–3¼ cups (14–16½ oz/440–515 g)
  unbleached bread flour, plus extra
  for top of loaf
¾ cup (4 oz/125 g) gluten flour
1 tablespoon salt
1 package (2¼ teaspoons) quick-rise
  yeast
2 cups (16 fl oz/500 ml) lukewarm
  water (110°F/43°C)
cornmeal for pan

Three risings give this free-form loaf an airy texture and a crisp crust.

❧

In a large bowl or the bowl of an electric stand mixer, combine 1 cup (5 oz/155 g) of the bread flour, the gluten flour, salt and yeast. Add the lukewarm water and stir well. Gradually stir in enough of the remaining flour to make a soft dough that holds its shape.

Knead by hand or with a dough hook, adding bread flour as necessary. Knead by hand until smooth and elastic, about 10 minutes; knead by hook until dough is not sticky and pulls cleanly from the bowl sides, 5–6 minutes. (See directions on pages 10–11.)

Form the dough into a ball and place in a clean, greased bowl, turning to grease all sides. Cover with plastic wrap and let rise in a warm place until doubled, 45–60 minutes.

Turn out the dough onto a lightly floured work surface and press flat. Knead for 1 minute, form into a ball and return to the greased bowl, turning the dough to grease all sides. Cover with plastic wrap and let rise again until doubled, 30–45 minutes.

Turn out the dough onto a lightly floured surface and press flat. Form into a ball, stretching the sides down and under, then form into a plump oval. Dust a baking sheet with cornmeal, place the loaf on it and cover with greased plastic wrap. Let rise until doubled, about 30 minutes. Preheat an oven to 400°F (200°C).

Uncover the loaf and sprinkle with bread flour. Using a sharp knife, make 3 diagonal cuts, each ½ inch (12 mm) deep, across the top. Using a spray bottle, spritz the oven sides and floor with water. Bake until the bread is brown, crusty and sounds hollow when tapped on the bottom, 30–35 minutes. Transfer the loaf to a wire rack to cool.

Makes one 1½-lb (750-g) oval loaf

Sourdough Olive Bread

1 teaspoon active dry yeast

½ cup (4 fl oz/125 ml) lukewarm water (110°F/43°C)

½ cup (3 oz/90 g) tapenade (*recipe on page 15*), at room temperature

2 cups (16 fl oz/500 ml) sourdough starter (*recipe on page 15*), at room temperature

½ teaspoon salt

3½–4 cups (17½–20 oz/545–625 g) unbleached bread flour

cornmeal for pans

1 egg white beaten with pinch of salt, for glaze

*I*n a large bowl or the bowl of an electric stand mixer, dissolve the yeast in the lukewarm water and let stand until bubbles start to rise, about 5 minutes. Stir in the tapenade, starter and salt. Gradually stir in 2½ cups (12½ oz/390 g) of the flour to make a soft dough that holds its shape.

Knead by hand or with a dough hook, adding flour as necessary. Knead by hand until smooth and elastic, about 10 minutes; knead by hook until dough is not sticky and pulls cleanly from the bowl sides, 5–6 minutes. (See directions on pages 10–11.) The dough will be slightly sticky.

Form the dough into a ball and place in a clean, greased bowl, turning to grease all sides. Cover with plastic wrap and let rise in a warm place until almost tripled, 1½–2 hours.

Line each of 2 double baguette pans (4 molds total), each 18 inches (45 cm) long and 6 inches (15 cm) wide, with a kitchen towel and sprinkle evenly with flour. Turn out the dough onto a floured work surface and press flat. Cut into 4 equal pieces, knead into balls and let rest for 5 minutes. Press each ball flat, fold into thirds and roll each into a 14-inch (35-cm) tapered rope. Place in the towel-lined pans. Cover with a kitchen towel; let rise until doubled, about 30 minutes. Preheat an oven to 450°F (230°C).

Place a shallow pan of boiling water on the floor of the preheated oven. Pull the pans out from under the towels. Grease the pans and sprinkle with cornmeal. One at a time, flip the loaves into the pans, underside up. Brush with the glaze. Using a sharp knife, make 3 curved slashes, each ½ inch (12 mm) deep, in each loaf. Bake until brown and crusty, 20–25 minutes. Transfer the loaves to a wire rack to cool.

Makes four ½-lb (250-g) baguettes

Potato Bread

2 baking potatoes, about ½ lb (250 g) total weight, peeled and quartered

1 package (2¼ teaspoons) quick-rise yeast

3½–4 cups (17½–20 oz/545–625 g) unbleached bread flour

1 tablespoon corn oil

1½ teaspoons salt

*I*n a saucepan, combine the potatoes with water to cover. Bring to a boil and boil until tender, 20–25 minutes. Drain, reserving the water. Pass the potatoes through a ricer or mash with a potato masher until smooth; let cool. Meanwhile, pour ½ cup (4 fl oz/ 125 ml) of the potato water into a large bowl or the bowl of an electric stand mixer and let cool to lukewarm (110°F/43°C). Stir in the yeast and then 3 tablespoons of the flour. Let stand until bubbly, about 15 minutes.

Rewarm ½ cup (4 fl oz/125 ml) of the remaining potato water to lukewarm and add to the bowl along with the oil, salt, potato and 3 cups (15 oz/470 g) of the flour. Stir well. Gradually stir in enough of the remaining flour to make a soft dough.

Knead by hand or with a dough hook, adding flour as necessary. Knead by hand until smooth and elastic, about 10 minutes; knead by hook until dough is not sticky and pulls cleanly from the bowl sides, 5–6 minutes. (See directions on pages 10–11.)

Form the dough into a ball and place in a clean, greased bowl, turning to grease all sides. Cover with plastic wrap and let rise in a warm place until doubled, 1–1½ hours.

Grease and flour a baking sheet. Turn out the dough onto a lightly floured work surface, press flat and knead for 2 minutes. Form into a ball, stretching the sides down and under. Flatten into a round 10 inches (25 cm) in diameter and place on the prepared sheet. Cover with a kitchen towel and let rise until doubled, 30–40 minutes. Preheat an oven to 425°F (220°C).

Uncover the loaf and bake for 15 minutes, then reduce the heat to 375°F (190°C) and continue to bake until browned and the loaf sounds hollow when tapped on the bottom, 35–40 minutes. Transfer the loaf to a wire rack to cool.

Makes one 22-oz (685-g) loaf

Rye Bread *Very good*

2½ cups (7½ oz/235 g) rye flour

1–1½ cups (5–7½ oz/155–235 g) unbleached bread flour

1 cup (5 oz/155 g) whole-wheat (wholemeal) flour

2 teaspoons salt

2 teaspoons caraway seeds

1 package (2¼ teaspoons) quick-rise yeast

1½ cups (12 fl oz/375 ml) warm water (125°F/52°C)

1 tablespoon vegetable oil

⅓ cup (3 fl oz/80 ml) dark molasses

cornmeal for pan

1 egg yolk beaten with 1 teaspoon water, for glaze

Add Powdered garlic

Wonderful for savory, deli-style sandwiches, this robust, dark bread is also good topped with lox and a squeeze of lemon.

❦

*I*n a large bowl or the bowl of an electric stand mixer, combine the rye flour, ¾ cup (4 oz/125 g) of the bread flour and the whole-wheat flour. Add the salt, caraway seeds and yeast and mix well. In a glass measuring pitcher, stir together the warm water, vegetable oil and molasses. Pour the water mixture into the flour mixture and stir until smooth.

Knead by hand or with a dough hook, adding bread flour as necessary. Knead by hand until smooth and elastic, about 15 minutes; knead by hook until dough is springy and pulls cleanly from the bowl sides, about 10 minutes. (See directions on pages 10–11.) The dough will be heavy.

Form the dough into a ball and place in a clean, greased bowl, turning to grease all sides. Cover with plastic wrap and let rise in a warm place until doubled, 1–1½ hours.

Turn out the dough onto a lightly floured work surface and press flat. Cut in half and form each half into a ball, stretching the sides down and under. Cover with plastic wrap and let rest for 5 minutes. Flatten each ball slightly and roll into a tapered log about 10 inches (25 cm) long. Sprinkle a large, heavy baking sheet with cornmeal and place the loaves on it. Cover loosely with greased plastic wrap and let rise until doubled, 20–30 minutes. Preheat an oven to 375°F (190°C).

Brush the loaves with the glaze. Bake until browned and the loaves sound hollow when tapped on the bottoms, 25–30 minutes. Transfer the loaves to a wire rack to cool.

Makes two 18-oz (560-g) loaves — *can bake in bread pans*

Scandinavian Beer Bread

1 package (2¼ teaspoons) active dry
   yeast

¾ cup (6 fl oz/180 ml) lukewarm water
   (110°F/43°C)

1 cup (8 fl oz/250 ml) dark beer such
   as Guinness stout, warmed to 110°F
   (43°C)

1 teaspoon salt

2 cups (6 oz/185 g) rye flour

3–3½ cups (15–17½ oz/470–545 g)
   unbleached bread flour

¼ cup (2 oz/60 g) unsalted butter

¼ cup (2 fl oz/60 ml) dark corn syrup

1 egg white, well beaten, for glaze

This glossy, richly flavored rye bread is particularly good for open-faced sandwiches and as an accompaniment to hearty soups.

*I*n a large bowl or the bowl of an electric stand mixer, dissolve the yeast in the lukewarm water and let stand until bubbles start to rise, about 5 minutes. Stir in the beer, salt, rye flour and 1 cup (5 oz/155 g) of the bread flour. Cover with a kitchen towel and let stand in a warm place for 1 hour.

In a small pan over low heat, melt the butter and add the corn syrup. Let cool to lukewarm (110°F/43°C), then add to the yeast-flour mixture. Gradually stir in 1½ cups (7½ oz/235 g) more bread flour to make a stiff but workable dough. Cover with greased plastic wrap and let rest for 30 minutes.

Knead by hand or with a dough hook, adding bread flour as necessary. Knead by hand until smooth and elastic, about 15 minutes; knead by hook until dough is not sticky and pulls cleanly from the bowl sides, about 10 minutes. (See directions on pages 10–11.)

Form the dough into a ball and place in a clean, greased bowl, turning to grease all sides. Cover with plastic wrap and let rise until doubled, 60–75 minutes.

Lightly flour a baking sheet. Turn out the dough onto a floured work surface and press flat. Cut in half and form each half into a ball, stretching the sides down and under, then flatten slightly. Place on the prepared baking sheet. Cover with a kitchen towel and let rise until doubled, 45–60 minutes.

Preheat an oven to 350°F (180°C). Brush the loaves with the glaze. Bake until browned and the loaves sound hollow when tapped on the bottoms, 35–40 minutes. Wrap in kitchen towels to promote a soft crust and place on a wire rack to cool.

Makes two 14-oz (440-g) loaves

Three-Grain Bread

2–2½ cups (10–12½ oz/315–390 g) unbleached bread flour

1 package (2¼ teaspoons) active dry yeast

2 cups (16 fl oz/500 ml) lukewarm water (110°F/43°C)

2 tablespoons corn oil

2 tablespoons dark or light molasses

2 teaspoons salt

2 cups (10 oz/315 g) whole-wheat (wholemeal) flour

½ cup (1½ oz/45 g) rye flour

½ cup (2½ oz/75 g) oat bran

2 teaspoons aniseeds

Serve this aromatic loaf with butter and preserves at breakfast, or use it for tuna or ham sandwiches.

In a large bowl or the bowl of an electric stand mixer, combine ¼ cup (1½ oz/45 g) of the bread flour, the yeast and ½ cup (4 fl oz/125 ml) of the lukewarm water and mix well. Let stand until bubbly, about 10 minutes. In a small bowl, stir together the remaining 1½ cups (12 fl oz/375 ml) lukewarm water, oil, molasses and salt. Add this mixture to the yeast mixture and stir well. Stir in 1½ cups (7½ oz/235 g) more bread flour, the whole-wheat flour, the rye flour and the oat bran. Add the aniseeds and stir briefly to mix.

Knead by hand or with a dough hook, adding bread flour as necessary. Knead by hand until smooth and elastic, about 15 minutes; knead by hook until dough is not sticky and pulls cleanly from the bowl sides, about 10 minutes. (See directions on pages 10–11.)

Form the dough into a ball and place in a clean, greased bowl, turning to grease all sides. Cover with plastic wrap and let rise in a warm place until doubled, 1½–2 hours.

Butter two 8½-by-4½-inch (21.5-by-11.5-cm) loaf pans. Turn out the dough onto a lightly floured work surface and press flat. Cut in half. Using a rolling pin, roll out each half into a 12-by-7-inch (30-by-18-cm) rectangle. Starting from a short side, roll up each like a jelly roll. Pinch the seams to seal and place in the prepared pans, seam sides down. Cover with a kitchen towel and let rise in a warm place until doubled, about 1 hour.

Preheat an oven to 375°F (190°C). Uncover and bake until browned and the loaves sound hollow when tapped on the bottoms, about 1 hour. Transfer the loaves to a wire rack to cool.

Makes two 1¼-lb (625-g) loaves

Polenta and Chestnut Flour Bread

1 cup (8 fl oz/250 ml) water

½ cup (3 oz/90 g) polenta, plus extra for pan

1 cup (8 fl oz/250 ml) milk

1 tablespoon corn oil

1 cup (3½ oz/105 g) chestnut flour, plus extra for dusting loaves

1 package (2¼ teaspoons) quick-rise yeast

½ cup (4 fl oz/125 ml) lukewarm water (110°F/43°C)

2 teaspoons salt

2 tablespoons dark brown sugar

3–3½ cups (15–17½ oz/470–545 g) unbleached bread flour

*I*n a saucepan over medium heat, bring the water to a boil. Pour in the polenta, stirring vigorously. Cook, stirring, until thickened, about 5 minutes. Spoon into a large bowl or the bowl of an electric stand mixer. Stir in the milk and oil. Let cool to lukewarm (110°F/43°C). Meanwhile, in a frying pan over medium heat, toast the 1 cup (3½ oz/105 g) chestnut flour, stirring until tan and fragrant, about 3 minutes. Let cool.

In a small bowl, dissolve the yeast in the water; let stand until bubbles start to rise, about 5 minutes. Stir the yeast mixture, salt, brown sugar and chestnut flour into the polenta. Gradually stir in 3 cups (15 oz/470 g) of the bread flour to make a soft dough.

Knead by hand or with a dough hook, adding bread flour as necessary. Knead by hand until smooth and elastic, about 10 minutes; knead by hook until dough is not sticky and pulls cleanly from the bowl sides, 5–6 minutes. (See directions on pages 10–11.) The dough will be slightly heavy.

Form the dough into a ball and place in a clean, greased bowl, turning to grease all sides. Cover with plastic wrap and let rise in a warm place until doubled, 1¼–1¾ hours.

Dust the work surface with chestnut flour. Turn out the dough and press flat. Cut in half, knead briefly and form each half into a ball, stretching the sides down and under. Elongate into two 8-by-3-inch (20-by-7.5-cm) ovals. Roll in chestnut flour. Dust a baking sheet with polenta and place the loaves on it. Cover with a kitchen towel and let rise until doubled, 45–60 minutes.

Preheat an oven to 425°F (220°C). Using a sharp knife, slash a grid pattern across each loaf. Bake for 10 minutes, then reduce the heat to 350°F (180°C) and bake until browned and the loaves sound hollow when tapped on the bottoms, 25–30 minutes. Transfer the loaves to a wire rack to cool.

Makes two 1¼-lb (625-g) loaves

Great —
good Taste
good texture

Old English Oatmeal Bread

These golden brown, oat-sprinkled round loaves are based on an old English country recipe.

1 cup (3 oz/90 g) old-fashioned rolled
    oats, plus extra for tops of loaves
¾ cup (6 fl oz/180 ml) milk
¾ cup (6 fl oz/180 ml) water
¼ cup (2 oz/60 g) unsalted butter
1 tablespoon dark molasses
2–2½ cups (10–12½ oz/315–390 g)
    unbleached bread flour
1 teaspoon salt
1 package (2½ teaspoons) quick-rise
    yeast
1 ~~egg yolk mixed with 1 teaspoon~~
    ~~water, for glaze~~
Browns too fast

*P*lace the 1 cup (3 oz/90 g) oats in a large bowl or the bowl of an electric stand mixer. In a saucepan over low heat, combine the milk, water and butter and bring to a boil. Pour over the oats and let stand until lukewarm (110°F/43°C), about 30 minutes; stir often to hasten cooling. Stir in the molasses, 1½ cups (7½ oz/ 235 g) of the flour, salt and yeast. Gradually stir in enough of the remaining flour to make a soft dough that holds its shape.

Knead by hand or with a dough hook, adding flour as necessary. Knead by hand until smooth and elastic, about 10 minutes; knead by hook until dough is not sticky and pulls cleanly from the bowl sides, 6–7 minutes. (See directions on pages 10–11.)

Form the dough into a ball and place in a clean, greased bowl, turning to grease all sides. Cover with plastic wrap and let rise in a warm place until doubled, 45–60 minutes.

Lightly flour a heavy baking sheet. Turn out the dough onto a lightly floured work surface and press flat. Cut in half, knead briefly and form each half into a ball, stretching the sides down and under. Place well apart on the prepared baking sheet and flatten slightly. Cover loosely with greased plastic wrap and let rise until doubled, 20–30 minutes.

Preheat an oven to 425°F (220°C).

Uncover the loaves, brush with the glaze and sprinkle with oats. Bake until golden brown and the loaves sound hollow when tapped on the bottoms, 25–30 minutes. Unmold the loaves and transfer to a wire rack to cool.

Makes two 13-oz (410-g) loaves

Swedish Limpa

2 cups (6 oz/185 g) rye flour

4–4½ cups (20–22½ oz/625–700 g) unbleached bread flour

1 teaspoon salt

1 teaspoon aniseeds

seeds from 12 cardamom pods, crushed (*see glossary, page 104*)

1 package (2¼ teaspoons) quick-rise yeast

¼ cup (2 oz/60 g) unsalted butter

1 cup (8 fl oz/250 ml) milk

1 cup (8 fl oz/250 ml) lukewarm water (110°F/43°C)

2 tablespoons dark corn syrup

A mainstay in Sweden, these flat, light brown loaves are cut into wedges and then split for serving plain with butter or as a base for sandwiches.

❧

In a large bowl or the bowl of an electric stand mixer, combine the rye flour, 3½ cups (17½ oz/545 g) of the bread flour, salt, aniseeds, cardamom and yeast. In a saucepan over low heat, combine the butter and milk. Heat briefly, stirring, until lukewarm (110°F/43°C). Add the lukewarm water and corn syrup. Stir the milk mixture into the flour mixture.

Knead by hand or with a dough hook, adding bread flour as necessary. Knead by hand until smooth and elastic, about 15 minutes; knead by hook until dough is not sticky and pulls cleanly from the bowl sides, about 10 minutes. (See directions on pages 10–11.)

Form the dough into a ball and place in a clean, greased bowl, turning to grease all sides. Cover with plastic wrap and let rise in a warm place until doubled, 45–60 minutes.

Turn out the dough onto a lightly floured work surface and press flat. Cut in half and form each half into a ball, stretching the sides down and under. Cover with a kitchen towel and let rest for 10 minutes. Dust a baking sheet with bread flour. Flatten each ball into a round 9 inches (23 cm) in diameter and place them on the prepared sheet. Cover and let rise until doubled, 35–45 minutes. Preheat an oven to 350°F (180°C).

Prick the loaves all over with a fork at 2-inch (5-cm) intervals. Bake until golden brown and the loaves sound hollow when tapped on the bottoms, 35–40 minutes. Using a spray bottle, mist the tops of the loaves with water. Wrap in kitchen towels to promote a soft crust and place on a wire rack to cool.

Makes two 1¼-lb (625-g) loaves

German Pumpernickel Bread

3 cups (9 oz/280 g) rye flour

1 cup (3 oz/90 g) wheat bran

about 3 cups (15 oz/370 g) unbleached bread flour

1 package (2¼ teaspoons) quick-rise yeast

½ cup (4 fl oz/125 ml) lukewarm water (110°F/43°C)

2 tablespoons dark or light molasses

3 tablespoons corn oil

2 teaspoons salt

2 cups (1 lb/500 g) plain low-fat yogurt, warmed to 110°F (43°C)

cornmeal for pan

Full of character, pumpernickel goes well with cheese and beer. It will keep for a week tightly wrapped in the refrigerator.

❧

*I*n a bowl, mix together the rye flour, wheat bran and 2 cups (10 oz/315 g) of the bread flour. In a large bowl or the bowl of an electric stand mixer, combine the yeast, ½ cup (2 oz/60 g) of the flour mixture and the lukewarm water; let stand until frothy, about 10 minutes. Stir in the molasses, oil and salt and then the yogurt. Gradually stir in 4 cups (1 lb/500g) of the remaining flour mixture to make a stiff but workable dough. The dough will be sticky.

Knead by hand or with a dough hook, adding the remaining flour mixture and then more bread flour as necessary. Knead by hand until smooth and elastic, about 15 m̈inutes; knead by hook until dough is not sticky and pulls cleanly from the bowl sides, about 10 minutes. (See directions on pages 10–11.) The dough will be slightly heavy.

Form the dough into a ball and place in a clean, greased bowl, turning to grease all sides. Cover with plastic wrap and let rise in a warm place until doubled, 60–75 minutes.

Turn out the dough onto a lightly floured work surface and press flat. Cut in half, knead briefly and form each half into a ball, stretching the sides down and under. Sprinkle a baking sheet with cornmeal and place the loaves on it. Cover with a kitchen towel and let rise until doubled, 45–60 minutes.

Preheat an oven to 350°F (180°C).

Uncover the loaves and bake until browned and the loaves sound hollow when tapped on the bottoms, about 1 hour. Transfer the loaves to a wire rack to cool.

Makes two 21-oz (655-g) loaves

Honey and Bran Loaf

1 package (2¼ teaspoons) quick-rise
  yeast
2½ cups (20 fl oz/625 ml) lukewarm
  water (110°F/43°C)
3 cups (15 oz/470 g) whole-wheat
  (wholemeal) flour
2–2½ cups (10–12½ oz/315–390 g)
  unbleached bread flour
2 cups (5 oz/155 g) wheat bran
¼ cup (3 oz/90 g) honey
1 tablespoon corn oil
1½ teaspoons salt
1 egg yolk beaten with 1 teaspoon
  water, for glaze

*Unlike typical high-fiber loaves, which can be dense and heavy, this
bread is quite light in texture and has a delicate, nutty flavor.*

☙

*I*n a small bowl, dissolve the yeast in ½ cup (4 fl oz/125 ml) of
the lukewarm water and let stand until bubbles start to rise,
about 5 minutes. In a large bowl or the bowl of an electric stand
mixer, combine the whole-wheat flour, 1 cup (5 oz/155 g) of
the bread flour and the bran. Stir in the remaining 2 cups (16 fl
oz/500 ml) lukewarm water, honey, oil, salt and yeast mixture.
Gradually stir in enough of the remaining bread flour to make
a soft dough that holds its shape.

Knead by hand or with a dough hook, adding bread flour as
necessary. Knead by hand until smooth and elastic, about
10 minutes; knead by hook until dough is not sticky and pulls
cleanly from the bowl sides, 6–7 minutes. (See directions on
pages 10–11.)

Form the dough into a ball and place in a clean, greased bowl,
turning the dough to grease all sides. Cover with plastic wrap and
let rise in a warm place until doubled, 45–60 minutes.

Grease two 8½-by-4½-inch (21.5-by-11.5-cm) loaf pans. Turn
out the dough onto a lightly floured work surface and press flat.
Cut in half. Using a rolling pin, roll out each half into a 12-by-
7-inch (30-by-18-cm) rectangle. Starting from a short side, roll
up each like a jelly roll. Pinch the seams to seal and place in the
prepared pans, seam sides down. Cover with a kitchen towel
and let rise in a warm place until doubled, 45–60 minutes.

Preheat an oven to 375°F (190°C).

Brush the loaves with the glaze. Bake until well browned and
the loaves sound hollow when tapped on the bottoms, about
35 minutes. Transfer the loaves to a wire rack to cool.

Makes two 23-oz (735-g) loaves

Whole-Wheat Bread

4½ cups (22½ oz/705 g) whole-wheat (wholemeal) flour

2½–3 cups (12½–15 oz/390–470 g) unbleached bread flour

2 teaspoons salt

1 package (2¼ teaspoons) quick-rise yeast

1 cup (8 fl oz/250 ml) water

1 cup (8 fl oz/250 ml) milk

¼ cup (2 fl oz/60 ml) dark molasses

¼ cup (2 oz/60 g) unsalted butter

1 egg yolk beaten with 1 teaspoon water, for glaze

A mixture of whole-wheat and unbleached white flour gives lighter results than an all whole-wheat loaf.

❧

*I*n a bowl, mix together the whole-wheat flour and 2½ cups (12½ oz/390 g) of the bread flour. In a large bowl or the bowl of an electric stand mixer, combine 2 cups (10 oz/315 g) of the flour mixture, the salt and yeast. In a pan over low heat, combine the water, milk, molasses and butter. Heat to lukewarm (110°F/43°C). Stir the water mixture into the flour-yeast mixture, then beat hard until smooth. Gradually stir in the remaining flour mixture.

Knead by hand or with a dough hook, adding bread flour as necessary. Knead by hand until smooth and elastic, about 10 minutes; knead by hook until dough is not sticky and pulls cleanly from the bowl sides, 6–7 minutes. (See directions on pages 10–11.) The dough will be slightly heavy.

Form into a ball and place in a clean, greased bowl, turning the dough to grease all sides. Cover with plastic wrap and let rise in a warm place until doubled, 1–1½ hours.

Grease two 8½-by-4½-inch (21.5-by-11.5-cm) loaf pans. Turn out the dough onto a lightly floured work surface and press flat. Cut in half. Using a rolling pin, roll out each half into a 12-by-7-inch (30-by-18-cm) rectangle. Starting from a short side, roll up each like a jelly roll. Pinch the seams to seal and place in the prepared pans, seam sides down. Cover with greased plastic wrap and let rise in a warm place until doubled, 45–60 minutes.

Preheat an oven to 375°F (190°C).

Brush the loaves with the glaze. Bake until golden brown and the loaves sound hollow when tapped on the bottoms, 30–40 minutes. Transfer the loaves to a wire rack to cool.

Makes two 22-oz (685-g) loaves

Russian-Style Black Bread

2¼ cups (6½ oz/200 g) rye flour

2¾–3¼ cups (14–16½ oz/440–515 g) unbleached bread flour

1 teaspoon sugar

1 teaspoon salt

¾ cup (2 oz/60 g) wheat bran

2 tablespoons unsweetened cocoa

1½ teaspoons caraway seeds, crushed

1 teaspoon fennel seeds, crushed

1 package (2¼ teaspoons) quick-rise yeast

1½ cups (12 fl oz/375 ml) water

1 tablespoon red wine vinegar

3 tablespoons dark molasses

¼ cup (2 oz/60 g) unsalted butter

1 teaspoon cornstarch (cornflour) dissolved in ½ cup (4 fl oz/125 ml) water, for glaze

*I*n a bowl, mix together the rye flour and 2¾ cups (14 oz/440 g) of the bread flour. In a large bowl or the bowl of an electric stand mixer, combine 1 cup (4 oz/120 g) of the flour mixture, the sugar, salt, bran, cocoa, caraway seeds, fennel seeds and yeast.

In a pan over low heat, combine the water, vinegar, molasses and butter. Heat to lukewarm (110°F/43°C); the butter need not melt entirely. Stir into the bran mixture. Add ½ cup (2 oz/60 g) of the flour mixture and beat until smooth. Gradually stir in the remaining flour mixture to make a stiff dough.

Knead by hand or with a dough hook, adding bread flour as necessary. Knead by hand until smooth and elastic, about 15 minutes; knead by hook until dough is springy and pulls cleanly from the bowl sides, about 10 minutes. (See directions on pages 10–11.) The dough will be heavy and slightly sticky.

Form the dough into a ball and place in a clean, greased bowl, turning to grease all sides. Cover with plastic wrap and let rise in a warm place until doubled, 45–60 minutes.

Grease two 8-inch (20-cm) round cake pans. Turn out the dough onto a lightly floured work surface and press flat. Knead for 1 minute. Cut in half and form each half into a 6-inch (15-cm) round, stretching the sides down and under. Place in the prepared pans. Cover with a kitchen towel and let rise until doubled, 40–50 minutes.

Preheat an oven to 350°F (180°C). Bake the loaves for 45 minutes. Mix the glaze in a pan, place over medium heat and cook, stirring, until it boils, turns clear and thickens, about 1 minute. Remove the loaves from the oven, then remove from the pans. Brush with the glaze and return to the oven, placing the loaves directly on the rack. Bake until the glaze sets and the loaves are browned and sound hollow when tapped on the bottoms, about 3 minutes longer. Transfer the loaves to a wire rack to cool.

Makes two 1-lb (500-g) loaves

Portuguese Corn Bread

1 cup (5 oz/150 g) yellow cornmeal,
  plus extra for pan
1 teaspoon salt
1 cup (8 fl oz/250 ml) boiling water
1 tablespoon corn oil
1½–2 cups (7½–10 oz/235–315 g)
  unbleached bread flour
1½ teaspoons quick-rise yeast

Unlike American corn bread, the Portuguese variety is baked in large, round loaves. It's delicious offered alongside a hearty soup.

*I*n a large bowl or the bowl of an electric stand mixer, combine ½ cup (2½ oz/75 g) of the cornmeal, the salt and boiling water. Stir until smooth. Stir in the corn oil and let cool to lukewarm (110°F/43°C). Stir in the remaining ½ cup (2½ oz/75 g) cornmeal, ½ cup (2½ oz/75 g) of the flour and the yeast. Cover with plastic wrap and let rise in a warm place until doubled, 30–45 minutes.

Stir to deflate the dough and gradually stir in 1 cup (5 oz/155 g) more flour.

Knead by hand or with a dough hook, adding flour as necessary. Knead by hand until smooth and elastic, about 10 minutes; knead by hook until dough is not sticky and pulls cleanly from the bowl sides, 6–7 minutes. (See directions on pages 10–11.) The dough should be firm but not stiff.

Form the dough into a ball, stretching the sides down and under. Sprinkle a heavy baking sheet with cornmeal and place the dough on it. Cover loosely with greased plastic wrap and let rise until doubled, 45–60 minutes.

Preheat an oven to 375°F (190°C).

Uncover the loaf and place the baking sheet in the oven. Using a spray bottle, spritz the oven floor and sides with water (this creates steam to help form a crisp crust). Bake until golden brown and the loaf sounds hollow when tapped on the bottom, 35–45 minutes. Transfer the loaf to a wire rack to cool.

Makes one 15-oz (470-g) loaf

Round Currant Loaf

about 2½ cups (12½ oz/390 g)
   unbleached bread flour
¼ cup (2 oz/60 g) sugar
½ teaspoon salt
¼ teaspoon ground cloves
¼ teaspoon ground cinnamon
1½ teaspoons quick-rise yeast
½ cup (4 fl oz/125 ml) milk
½ cup (4 fl oz/125 ml) water
2 tablespoons unsalted butter, plus
   extra for greasing
1 egg, at room temperature
½ cup (3 oz/90 g) dried currants or
   raisins

Lightly spiced and studded with tiny currants, this round bread is excellent toasted and spread with butter for a morning or afternoon treat. If you would like to make more than one loaf at a time, the recipe can easily be doubled.

❧

*I*n a bowl, combine 1½ cups (7½ oz/235 g) of the flour, the sugar, salt, cloves, cinnamon and yeast. In a saucepan over low heat, combine the milk, water and the 2 tablespoons butter. Heat briefly, stirring often, until lukewarm (110°F/43°C). Stir the milk mixture into the flour mixture, then beat with an electric mixer set on medium speed or beat hard with a wooden spoon until smooth, about 2 minutes, scraping down the sides of the bowl occasionally. Add the egg and ½ cup (2½ oz/75 g) more flour. Beat at high speed or hard by hand until smooth, about 2 minutes. Gradually stir in enough of the remaining flour to make a batter that almost holds its shape. (If too stiff, stir in a little warm water.) Cover with greased plastic wrap and let rise in a warm place until doubled, 1–1½ hours.

Butter a 1-qt (1-l) porcelain soufflé dish, tinned steel charlotte mold or any round 1-qt (1-l) mold. Uncover the bowl and stir the batter to deflate. Stir in the currants or raisins. Spoon the batter into the prepared mold and smooth the top with a rubber spatula. Cover loosely with greased plastic wrap and let rise until the bread reaches the top of the mold, 30–40 minutes.

Preheat an oven to 375°F (190°C).

Uncover the dough and bake until well browned and domed on top, 30–40 minutes. Unmold the loaf and transfer to a wire rack to cool.

Makes one 1½-lb (750-g) loaf

Irish Soda Bread

2¼ cups (11½ oz/360 g) unbleached
  bread flour, plus extra for dusting
½ cup (1½ oz/45 g) old-fashioned
  rolled oats
¼ cup (½ oz/15 g) wheat bran
1½ teaspoons baking soda (bicarbonate
  of soda)
1 teaspoon salt
¼ cup (2 oz/60 g) cold unsalted butter,
  cut into small pieces
1½ cups (12 oz/375 g) plain lowfat
  yogurt

Add currents

*The traditional bread of Ireland, this rustic loaf is wonderful sliced
and spread with butter for breakfast or afternoon tea. Irish wheat
flour is very soft; adding rolled oats and bran to the harder American
wheat flour helps to approximate the correct texture. The dough will
start rising as soon as the baking soda comes in contact with the
yogurt, so it must be mixed and formed quickly and baked at once.
Since soda bread is best when fresh, you may wish to make two
small loaves instead of one large one; bake the small loaves for
25 minutes only, and freeze one when cooled.*

ᴄ

Place a heavy baking sheet in the oven and preheat to 425°F
(220°C).

   In a large bowl, combine the 2¼ cups (11½ oz/360 g) flour,
the oats, bran, baking soda and salt. Add the butter and rub it
in with your fingertips until the mixture resembles coarse meal.
Add the yogurt and stir to blend as evenly as possible, forming
a rough ball.

   Turn out the dough onto a lightly floured work surface and
knead gently for about 30 seconds, dusting with just enough
flour to avoid sticking. The dough should be soft.

   Sprinkle a little flour on a clean work surface and set the ball
of dough on it. Flatten slightly into a 7-inch (18-cm) dome and
sprinkle with flour, spreading it lightly over the surface with
your fingertips. Using a sharp knife, cut a shallow X from one
side of the loaf to the other. Using a large spatula, transfer the
loaf to the preheated baking sheet and bake until well risen,
brown, crusty and the loaf sounds hollow when tapped on the
bottom, 30–35 minutes. Transfer the loaf to a wire rack to cool.

Makes one 1¼-lb (625-g) loaf

Walnut Bread

1 cup (5 oz/155 g) whole-wheat
  (wholemeal) flour

1¾–2 cups (9–10 oz/280–315 g)
  unbleached bread flour

½ teaspoon salt

1½ teaspoons quick-rise yeast

1 cup (8 fl oz/250 ml) warm water
  (125°F/52°C)

1 egg, at room temperature

1 tablespoon dark molasses

2 tablespoons walnut oil, plus extra
  for greasing

½ cup (2 oz/60 g) chopped walnuts

Scented with walnut oil and studded with chopped walnuts, this simple-to-make batter bread is delicious served in thin slices with a selection of cheeses.

In a large bowl, combine the whole-wheat flour, 1 cup (5 oz/ 155 g) of the bread flour, salt and yeast. In a small bowl, stir together the warm water, egg, molasses and the 2 tablespoons walnut oil. Stir the water mixture into the flour mixture. Using an electric mixer set on medium speed, beat until smooth, about 2 minutes. Gradually beat in enough of the remaining bread flour to form a batter that almost holds its shape. (If too stiff, stir in a little warm water.) Cover the bowl with greased plastic wrap and let rise in a warm place until doubled, 45–60 minutes.

Grease a 1-qt (1-l) tinned steel charlotte mold, porcelain soufflé dish or any round 1-qt (1-l) mold with walnut oil. Uncover the bowl and stir the batter to deflate. Stir in all but 2 tablespoons of the walnuts. Spoon the batter into the prepared mold and smooth the top with a rubber spatula. Scatter the walnuts evenly over the top. Cover with greased plastic wrap and let rise until doubled, 30–45 minutes.

Preheat an oven to 375°F (190°C).

Uncover the loaf and bake until golden brown, 30–40 minutes. Unmold the loaf and transfer to a wire rack to cool.

Makes one 1¼-lb (625-g) loaf

Rosemary Batter Bread

½ cup (2½ oz/75 g) whole-wheat
(wholemeal) flour

1¾–2 cups (9–10 oz/280–315 g)
unbleached bread flour

2 teaspoons salt

1 package (2¼ teaspoons) quick-rise
yeast

1 cup (8 fl oz/250 ml) warm water
(125°F/52°C)

2 tablespoons olive oil, plus extra for
greasing

1 egg, at room temperature

1 teaspoon chopped fresh rosemary

cornmeal for mold

2 teaspoons pine nuts

This savory batter bread goes well with simple, Mediterranean-style food, such as spit-roasted lamb, charbroiled poultry or fish steaks.

☙

*I*n a large bowl, combine the whole-wheat flour, 1 cup (5 oz/ 155 g) of the bread flour, salt and yeast and mix well. In a small bowl, stir together the warm water, the 2 tablespoons olive oil, the egg and rosemary. Stir the water mixture into the flour mixture, then beat with an electric mixer set on medium speed or beat hard with a wooden spoon until smooth, about 2 minutes, scraping down the sides of the bowl occasionally. Gradually beat in enough of the remaining bread flour to make a stiff batter that almost holds its shape. Beat at high speed or hard by hand until smooth, about 2 minutes. Cover with plastic wrap and let rise in a warm place until doubled, 40–50 minutes.

Grease a 1-qt (1-l) porcelain soufflé dish, tinned steel charlotte mold or any round 1-qt (1-l) mold with olive oil and sprinkle with cornmeal. Uncover the bowl and stir the batter to deflate. Spoon the batter into the prepared mold and smooth the top with a rubber spatula. Scatter the pine nuts evenly over the top. Cover loosely with greased plastic wrap and let rise until doubled, 30–45 minutes.

Preheat an oven to 375°F (190°C).

Uncover the dough and bake until golden and well risen, 35–40 minutes. (If the nuts start to overbrown, cover the loaf loosely with aluminum foil.) Unmold the loaf and transfer to a wire rack to cool.

Makes one 1¼-lb (625-g) loaf

Golden Sesame Breadsticks

3–3½ cups (15–17½ oz/470–545 g) unbleached bread flour

2 teaspoons salt

1 package (2¼ teaspoons) quick-rise yeast

1 cup (8 fl oz/250 ml) lukewarm water (110°F/43°C)

1 egg yolk beaten with 2 teaspoons water and ½ teaspoon salt, for glaze

1 cup (3 oz/90 g) sesame seeds

Crunchy breadsticks are good with salad, soup or a glass of wine.

✳

*I*n a large bowl or the bowl of an electric stand mixer, combine 2 cups (10 oz/315 g) of the flour, the salt and yeast. Stir in the lukewarm water. Gradually stir in enough of the remaining flour to make a soft dough that holds its shape.

Knead by hand or with a dough hook, adding flour as necessary. Knead by hand until smooth and elastic, about 10 minutes; knead by hook until dough is not sticky and pulls cleanly from the bowl sides, 6–7 minutes. (See directions on pages 10–11.)

Form the dough into a ball and place in a clean, greased bowl, turning to grease all sides. Cover with plastic wrap and let rise in a warm place until doubled, 45–60 minutes.

Turn out the dough onto a lightly floured work surface and press flat. Cover with a kitchen towel and let rest for 5 minutes. Grease 2 baking sheets. Using a rolling pin, roll out the dough into a 10-by-12-inch (25-by-30-cm) rectangle about ½ inch (12 mm) thick. Using a sharp knife, cut lengthwise into 20 strips, each ½ inch (12 mm) wide. Using the palms of your hands, roll and elongate to form ropes 14 inches (35 cm) long. Place on the prepared sheets about 1 inch (2.5 cm) apart, cover loosely with greased plastic wrap and let rise for 20 minutes.

Preheat an oven to 300°F (150°C).

Uncover and bake until lightly golden, about 25 minutes; switch pan positions halfway through baking. Transfer the breadsticks to a work surface. Brush with the glaze and sprinkle with sesame seeds on both sides. Return the breadsticks to the sheets. Continue to bake until deep gold and crisp, 14–17 minutes longer. Transfer the breadsticks to a wire rack to cool.

Makes twenty 14-inch (35-cm) breadsticks

63

English Muffins

3 cups (15 oz/470 g) unbleached bread
  flour

1½ teaspoons active dry yeast

¾ cup (6 fl oz/180 ml) plus 2 tablespoons lukewarm water (110°F/43°C)

2 teaspoons salt

1 teaspoon sugar

¾ cup (6 fl oz/180 ml) plus 2 tablespoons lukewarm milk (110°F/43°C)

2 tablespoons corn oil

brown-rice flour or cornmeal for muffin
  rings and griddle

If you do not have muffin rings, make them by folding 7-by-12-inch (18-by-30-cm) sheets of aluminum foil in half lengthwise, and then in thirds, forming 6 layers in all. Bend the strips into circles 3½ inches (9 cm) in diameter and secure with tape at the top.

Preheat an oven to 250°F (120°C). Place the flour in a large ovenproof bowl in the oven until warm to the touch, about 10 minutes. Meanwhile, dissolve the yeast in the lukewarm water and let stand until bubbles start to rise, about 5 minutes.

Add the salt and sugar to the warmed flour. Stir in the lukewarm milk, oil and yeast mixture and beat until smooth, making an almost pourable batter. Cover with plastic wrap and let rise in a warm place until doubled, 60–70 minutes.

Place a griddle (or 2 heavy frying pans) in the oven. Turn on the oven to its lowest setting, heat for 5 minutes, then switch off the heat. Remove the griddle or pans and sprinkle with the rice flour or cornmeal. Butter eight 3½-inch (9-cm) muffin rings on the inside and dip in rice flour or cornmeal to coat evenly. Arrange the rings on the griddle or the pans.

Stir the batter to deflate and scoop about ¼ cup (2 fl oz/60 ml) into each ring. Place the muffins in the still barely warm oven and let rise, uncovered, until almost doubled, about 30 minutes.

Set the griddle or pans over medium-low heat. Cook slowly, loosening the muffins with a spatula after 5 minutes to prevent sticking, until the bottoms are a very pale brown, 8–10 minutes. Gently remove the rings and turn the muffins over. Lightly brown on the second side, about 8 minutes.

Transfer the muffins to a wire rack to cool. Using a fork, split the muffins in half and then toast them.

Makes 8 muffins

Dinner Rolls

4½–5 cups (22½–25 oz/700–780 g)
    unbleached bread flour
2 teaspoons salt
1 package (2¼ teaspoons) quick-rise
    yeast
1½ cups (12 fl oz/375 ml) warm water
    (125°F/52°C)
¼ cup (2 oz/60 g) unsalted butter, at
    room temperature
cornmeal for pan
1 egg white beaten with 2 teaspoons
    cold water, for glaze
poppyseeds for tops of rolls

*The crisp exterior of these elegant bread rolls contrasts nicely with
their delicate crumb.*

*I*n a large bowl or the bowl of an electric stand mixer, combine
1 cup (5 oz/155 g) of the flour, the salt and yeast. Using a
wooden spoon or the paddle attachment of the mixer set on
medium speed, beat in the warm water and butter until smooth.
Add 1 cup (5 oz/155 g) more flour and continue beating until
smooth. Gradually beat in enough of the remaining flour to make
a soft dough that holds its shape.

Knead by hand or with a dough hook, adding flour as necessary. Knead by hand until smooth and elastic, about 10 minutes;
knead by hook until dough is not sticky and pulls cleanly from
the bowl sides, 6–7 minutes. (See directions on pages 10–11.)

Form the dough into a ball and place in a clean, greased bowl,
turning to grease all sides. Cover with plastic wrap and let rise
in a warm place until doubled, 45–60 minutes.

Turn out the dough onto a lightly floured work surface and
press flat. Form into a ball and let rest for 5 minutes. Cut the
dough in half. Roll each half into a log 9 inches (23 cm) long.
Cut crosswise into 9 equal pieces. Knead each piece into a ball.
Sprinkle 2 baking sheets with the cornmeal and place the rolls
on them, spaced well apart. Cover loosely with greased plastic
wrap and let rise until doubled, about 35 minutes.

Preheat an oven to 425°F (220°C).

Brush the rolls with the glaze and sprinkle with poppyseeds.
Using a spray bottle, spritz the oven sides and floor with water.
Bake until golden, 15–20 minutes; switch pan positions half-
way through baking. Transfer the rolls to a wire rack to cool.
Serve warm.

Makes 18 rolls

Scottish Oatcakes

1 cup (3 oz/90 g) old-fashioned rolled
  oats
⅓ cup (1½ oz/45 g) whole-wheat
  (wholemeal) flour
½ teaspoon sugar
¼ teaspoon salt
¼ teaspoon baking soda (bicarbonate
  of soda)
¼ cup (2 oz/60 g) cold unsalted butter,
  cut into pieces
2–3 tablespoons water

The traditional bread of Scotland, oatcakes are thinly rolled oatmeal crackers baked on a griddle. The authentic Highland oatcake is quite plain; this richer Border version (i.e., the border between Scotland and England) includes wheat flour and butter, and is oven baked. Serve oatcakes with Dundee marmalade or heather honey, or with cheese.

Preheat an oven to 325°F (165°C).

In a food processor fitted with the metal blade, process the oats to a fine meal. Add the whole-wheat flour, sugar, salt, baking soda and butter, and process briefly to mix well. With the motor running, add 2 tablespoons of the water and process for 20 seconds to form a crumbly dough, adding as much of the remaining 1 tablespoon water as needed to achieve the desired texture.

Turn out the dough onto a lightly floured work surface. Knead a couple of times to incorporate any crumbs, then form into a ball. Cut in half. Using a rolling pin, roll out each half into a round 6 inches (15 cm) in diameter and ¼ inch (6 mm) thick. Crimp the edges using your finger and thumb to make a fluted border. Using a metal spatula, transfer the rounds to a heavy baking sheet and cut each one into 4 equal wedges. Separate the wedges slightly, then prick the top of each one 3 or 4 times with a fork.

Bake until pale tan and no longer soft, 25–30 minutes. Transfer the oatcakes to a wire rack to cool.

Makes 8 oatcakes

Bagels

1 package (2¼ teaspoons) quick-rise
  yeast
2½–3 cups (12½–15 oz/390–470 g)
  unbleached bread flour
1 cup (8 fl oz/250 ml) lukewarm milk
  (110°F/43°C)
¼ cup (2 fl oz/60 ml) corn oil
1 teaspoon regular salt
1 egg, separated
1 tablespoon sugar
3 qt (3 l) water
poppyseeds, sesame seeds or coarse salt
  crystals for tops of bagels

These finely textured rolls are first poached and then baked.

✳

*I*n a large bowl or the bowl of an electric stand mixer, combine the yeast and ½ cup (2½ oz/75 g) of the flour. Stir in the milk and let stand until frothy, about 10 minutes. Using a wooden spoon, beat in the oil, regular salt, egg yolk and sugar. Gradually beat in enough of the remaining flour to make a firm dough.

Knead by hand or with a dough hook, adding flour as necessary. Knead by hand until smooth and elastic, about 10 minutes; knead by hook until dough is not sticky and pulls cleanly from the bowl sides, 6–7 minutes. (See directions on pages 10–11.)

Form the dough into a ball and place in a clean, greased bowl, turning to grease all sides. Cover with plastic wrap and let rise in a warm place until doubled, 45–60 minutes.

Turn out the dough onto a lightly floured work surface and press flat. Roll into a log about 8 inches (20 cm) long and cut into 16 equal pieces. Cover with a kitchen towel. One at a time, form each piece into a ball, then flatten it into a round 2½ inches (6 cm) in diameter. Using the handle of a wooden spoon, make a hole through the center of each round, then gently widen the hole to 1 inch (2.5 cm) in diameter. Place the rounds on the work surface, cover with the towel and let rise until doubled, about 20 minutes. Preheat an oven to 375°F (190°C). Grease a baking sheet.

In a pot, bring the water to a boil. Reduce the heat to low. Slip 3 bagels at a time into the simmering water. Poach, turning once, for 3 minutes on each side; reform the holes if necessary. Using a slotted spoon, transfer to the prepared sheet.

Lightly beat the egg white and brush over the bagels. Sprinkle with the seeds or coarse salt. Bake until golden brown, about 30 minutes. Transfer the bagels to wire racks to cool.

Makes 16 bagels

Currant Scones

-OK-

2 cups (10 oz/315 g) all-purpose (plain)
    flour, plus extra for dusting
1 teaspoon baking powder
¼ teaspoon salt
⅓ cup (2½ oz/75 g) sugar
¼ cup (2 oz/60 g) cold unsalted
    butter, cut into pieces
½ cup (3 oz/90 g) dried currants
½ cup (4 fl oz/125 ml) milk
1 egg yolk beaten with 1 teaspoon
    water, for glaze

Traditionally triangular in shape, these small Irish-Scottish cakes were at one time always cooked on a griddle. Delicious for breakfast or afternoon tea, scones are at their best served warm from the oven, split and spread with butter.

Preheat an oven to 375°F (190°C). Grease and flour a heavy baking sheet.

In a large bowl, sift together the 2 cups (10 oz/315 g) flour, the baking powder, salt and sugar. Using your fingertips, rub in the butter until the mixture resembles fine meal. Stir in the currants. Make a well in the center of the flour mixture and pour in the milk. Using a rubber spatula, quickly mix together to form a soft dough. (Do not overmix.)

Turn out the dough onto a lightly floured work surface and cut in half. Place each half well apart on the prepared baking sheet. Lightly form each half into a round about ½ inch (12 mm) thick. Brush the tops with the glaze. Then, using a sharp knife, score each round into 10 equal wedges, cutting about halfway through.

Bake until well risen and golden brown, 15–17 minutes. Transfer to a wire rack and let cool slightly, then cut apart. Serve warm.

Makes 20 scones

Scottish Floury Baps

3½–4 cups (17½–20 oz/545–625 g) unbleached bread flour, plus extra for dusting

1 teaspoon salt

1 package (2¼ teaspoons) quick-rise yeast

1 cup (8 fl oz/250 ml) milk

¼ cup (2 oz/60 g) unsalted butter

A traditional breakfast bread in Scotland, these soft, oval rolls always delight visitors to that country. Serve warm with butter and Dundee marmalade or heather honey.

In a large bowl or the bowl of an electric stand mixer, combine 3 cups (15 oz/470 g) of the flour, the salt and yeast. In a saucepan over low heat, combine the milk and butter. Heat briefly, stirring often, until warm (125°F/52°C). Make a well in the center of the flour mixture, pour in the milk mixture and stir until combined.

Knead by hand or with a dough hook, adding flour as necessary. Knead by hand until smooth and elastic, about 10 minutes; knead by hook until dough is not sticky and pulls cleanly from the bowl sides, 6–7 minutes. (See directions on pages 10–11.)

Form the dough into a ball and place in a clean, greased bowl, turning to grease all sides. Cover with plastic wrap and let rise in a warm place until doubled, 45–60 minutes.

Turn out the dough onto a lightly floured work surface and press flat. Let rest for 5 minutes. Roll into a log 10 inches (25 cm) long, then cut into 10 equal pieces. Knead each piece into a ball, then form each ball into an oval ½ inch (12 mm) thick. Lightly dust a heavy baking sheet with flour and place the rolls on it, spaced well apart. Cover loosely with greased plastic wrap and let rise until doubled, about 20 minutes. Preheat an oven to 425°F (220°C).

Uncover the rolls, press each one gently in the center with 3 fingers to prevent the tops from splitting, then sift a light dusting of flour over the tops. Bake until well risen and lightly browned, 15–18 minutes. Serve warm.

Makes 10 rolls

Sticky Buns

4½–5 cups (22½–25 oz/700–780 g) unbleached bread flour

½ cup (4 oz/125 g) granulated sugar

1 teaspoon salt

1 package (2¼ teaspoons) quick-rise yeast

½ cup (4 fl oz/125 ml) milk

½ cup (4 fl oz/125 ml) water

¾ cup (6 oz/180 g) unsalted butter, at room temperature

2 eggs, at room temperature

1 cup (7 oz/220 g) firmly packed brown sugar

1 teaspoon ground cinnamon

⅔ cup (4 oz/125 g) raisins

⅔ cup (2½ oz/75 g) coarsely chopped pecans

In a large bowl or the bowl of an electric stand mixer, combine 1½ cups (7½ oz/235 g) of the flour, the granulated sugar, salt and yeast. In a pan over low heat, combine the milk, water and ¼ cup (2 oz/60 g) of the butter and heat to lukewarm (110°F/ 43°C). Gradually beat the milk mixture into the flour mixture. Beat in the eggs, then gradually stir in 2½ cups (12½ oz/390 g) more flour to make a soft dough that holds its shape.

Knead by hand or with a dough hook, adding flour as necessary. Knead by hand until smooth and elastic, about 10 minutes; knead by hook until dough is not sticky and pulls cleanly from the bowl sides, 6–7 minutes. (See directions on pages 10–11.)

Form the dough into a ball and place in a clean, greased bowl, turning to grease all sides. Cover with plastic wrap and let rise in a warm place until doubled, 1¼–1¾ hours.

Turn out the dough onto a lightly floured work surface. Cut in half. Using a rolling pin, roll out each half into an 8-by-15-inch (20-by-37.5-cm) rectangle. Spread with ¼ cup (2 oz/60 g) of the remaining butter, dividing it equally. In a bowl, mix ½ cup (3½ oz/110 g) of the brown sugar, cinnamon and raisins, and sprinkle half of it over the dough. Starting from a long side, roll up tightly. Pinch the seams to seal. Cut each crosswise into 10 equal slices.

Butter one 9-inch (23-cm) round and one 8-inch (20-cm) square cake pan. Add the remaining ½ cup (3½ oz/110 g) brown sugar and ¼ cup (2 oz/60 g) butter to the remaining sugar mixture; stir well. Add the pecans and sprinkle over pan bottoms. Place 9 dough slices, cut sides down and almost touching, in the square pan. Place 11 dough slices in the round pan. Cover with a kitchen towel and let rise until doubled, 60–75 minutes.

Preheat an oven to 350°F (180°C). Uncover the loaves and bake until golden brown, 30–35 minutes. Invert the pans onto wire racks set over aluminum foil. Lift off the pans and serve warm.

Makes 2 pull-apart loaves, about 1½ lb (750 g) each

Focaccia

1 package (2¼ teaspoons) quick-rise
  yeast
1¼ cups (10 fl oz/310 ml) lukewarm
  water (110°F/43°C)
2 tablespoons olive oil, plus extra for
  top of loaf and pan
2 teaspoons regular salt
3–3½ cups (15–17½ oz/470–545 g)
  unbleached bread flour
coarse sea salt for top of loaf

*This flat Italian bread is delectable served warm from the oven with
cheese and a glass of wine. Or split it for making great sandwiches.
It is best eaten on the day it's made.*

*I*n a large bowl or the bowl of an electric stand mixer, dissolve
the yeast in the lukewarm water. Stir in the 2 tablespoons olive
oil and the regular salt. Gradually stir in 3 cups (15 oz/470 g) of
the flour to make a soft dough that holds its shape.

Knead by hand or with a dough hook, adding flour as necessary. Knead by hand until smooth and elastic, about 10 minutes;
knead by hook until dough is not sticky and pulls cleanly from
the bowl sides, 6–7 minutes. (See directions on pages 10–11.)

Form the dough into a ball and place in a clean, greased bowl,
turning to grease all sides. Cover with plastic wrap and let rise
in a warm place until doubled, 45–60 minutes.

Grease an 11-by-17-inch (28-by-43-cm) heavy baking sheet
with 1-inch (2.5-cm) sides with olive oil. Turn out the dough
onto a lightly floured work surface and press flat. Form into a
ball. Place on the prepared baking sheet; let rest for 5 minutes.
Using your fingers, stretch out the dough so that it evenly covers
the pan bottom. Cover with a kitchen towel and let rise until
puffy, about 30 minutes. Preheat an oven to 400°F (200°C).

Uncover the dough and, using your fingertips, make a pattern
of dimples at 2-inch (5-cm) intervals over the entire surface.
Brush the surface with olive oil and lightly sprinkle with sea salt.

Bake until golden brown, 15–20 minutes. Cut into pieces and
serve warm.

Makes one 1-lb (500-g) flat bread

Crusty Corn Focaccia

1 cup (5 oz/155 g) brown-rice flour

1 cup (5½ oz/170 g) corn flour, plus extra for tops of loaves

½ cup (2 oz/60 g) cornstarch (cornflour)

1 teaspoon salt

2 teaspoons xanthan gum powder

1½ teaspoons active dry yeast

1½ cups (12 fl oz/375 ml) warm water (125°F/52°C)

2 eggs, at room temperature

2 tablespoons corn oil

1 egg yolk mixed with 1 teaspoon water, for glaze

This bread is a delicious alternative for those who cannot tolerate wheat. As neither corn flour (a finer-grind version of yellow cornmeal) nor brown-rice flour contains gluten, xanthan gum powder—a natural carbohydrate derived from corn syrup—is added to provide "stretch" and texture. All three products can be found in natural-food stores or in mail-order catalogs specializing in flours and grains.

Line a heavy baking sheet with parchment paper and set aside. In a large bowl, mix together the rice flour, the 1 cup (5½ oz/170 g) corn flour, cornstarch, salt, xanthan gum powder and yeast. In a separate bowl, stir together the warm water, eggs and corn oil. Pour the water mixture onto the flour mixture and beat with a wooden spoon until smooth.

Using a rubber spatula, spread the dough into 2 circles, each 8 inches (20 cm) in diameter, on the prepared baking sheet, mounding them slightly in the center. Cover loosely with greased plastic wrap and let rise in a warm place until doubled, 1–1½ hours.

Preheat an oven to 425°F (220°C).

Uncover the dough and brush with the glaze. Sprinkle with corn flour and, using a sharp knife or single-edged razor blade, slash the dough with a 2-inch (5-cm) diamond-grid pattern.

Bake until light golden brown, 14–18 minutes. Transfer the loaves to a wire rack to cool. Cut into pieces before serving.

Makes two 10-oz (315-g) loaves

Focaccia with Pancetta

1 package (2¼ teaspoons) quick-rise
  yeast
½ cup (4 fl oz/125 ml) lukewarm water
  (110°F/43°C)
¾ cup (6 fl oz/180 ml) lukewarm milk
  (110°F/43°C)
1 tablespoon olive oil, plus extra for pan
1 teaspoon salt
3½–4 cups (17½–20 oz/545–625 g)
  unbleached bread flour
¼ lb (125 g) pancetta, diced, lightly
  fried, drained and cooled

This tasty bread, which contains little nuggets of pancetta (Italian bacon), tastes best served warm from the oven.

*I*n a large bowl or the bowl of an electric stand mixer, dissolve the yeast in the water. Stir in the lukewarm milk, the 1 tablespoon oil and the salt. Gradually stir in 3 cups (15 oz/470 g) of the flour to make a soft dough that holds its shape.

Knead by hand or with a dough hook, adding flour as necessary. Knead by hand until smooth and elastic, about 10 minutes; knead by hook until dough is not sticky and pulls cleanly from the bowl sides, 6–7 minutes. (See directions on pages 10–11.)

Form the dough into a ball and place in a clean, greased bowl, turning to grease all sides. Cover with plastic wrap and let rise in a warm place until doubled, 45–60 minutes.

Grease an 11-by-17-inch (28-by-43-cm) baking sheet with 1-inch (2.5-cm) sides with olive oil. Turn out the dough onto a lightly floured work surface and press flat. Sprinkle with the pancetta and knead gently to distribute evenly. Form into a ball and place on the prepared sheet. Cover loosely with plastic wrap and let rest for 10 minutes. With your fingers, stretch out the dough so that it evenly covers the pan bottom. Cover with a kitchen towel and let rise until puffy, 45–60 minutes.

Preheat an oven to 400°F (200°C).

Uncover the dough and, using your fingertips, make a pattern of dimples at 2-inch (5-cm) intervals over the entire surface. Bake until golden brown, 15–17 minutes. Cut into pieces and serve warm.

Makes one 1½-lb (750-g) flat bread

Focaccia with Onions

1 package (2¼ teaspoons) quick-rise yeast

1¼ cups (10 fl oz/310 ml) lukewarm water (110°F/43°C)

3 tablespoons olive oil, plus extra for pan

2½ teaspoons salt

3–3½ cups (15–17½ oz/470–545 g) unbleached bread flour

½ cup (4 oz/125 g) unsalted butter

2 lb (1 kg) mild yellow onions, thinly sliced

1 teaspoon sugar

Topped with golden, buttery onions, this flavorful flat bread makes a delicious warm snack with a glass of wine.

*I*n a large bowl or the bowl of an electric stand mixer, dissolve the yeast in the lukewarm water. Stir in the 3 tablespoons oil and 2 teaspoons of the salt. Gradually stir in 3 cups (15 oz/470 g) of the flour to make a soft dough that holds its shape.

Knead by hand or with a dough hook, adding flour as necessary. Knead by hand until smooth and elastic, about 10 minutes; knead by hook until dough is not sticky and pulls cleanly from the bowl sides, 6–7 minutes. (See directions on pages 10–11.)

Form the dough into a ball and place in a clean, greased bowl, turning to grease all sides. Cover with plastic wrap and let rise in a warm place until doubled, 45–60 minutes.

In 2 sauté pans over medium-low heat, melt the butter, dividing it equally. Add half of the onions to each pan and season with the sugar and the remaining ½ teaspoon salt. Cook, stirring, until soft but not browned, about 10 minutes. Let cool.

Grease an 11-by-17-inch (28-by-43-cm) baking sheet with 1-inch (2.5-cm) sides with olive oil. Turn out the dough onto a lightly floured work surface and press flat. Form into a ball, place on the prepared baking sheet and let rest for 5 minutes. Using your fingers, stretch the dough so that it evenly covers the pan bottom. Cover with a kitchen towel and let rise until puffy, 45–60 minutes.

Preheat an oven to 400°F (200°C). Using your fingertips, make a pattern of dimples at 2-inch (5-cm) intervals over the entire surface of the dough. Cover the surface with the sliced onions.

Bake until the crust is golden brown, 15–17 minutes. Cut into pieces and serve warm.

Makes one 1½-lb (750-g) flat bread

Sweet Focaccia with Grapes

1 package (2¼ teaspoons) quick-rise
  yeast

1½ cups (12 fl oz/375 ml) lukewarm
  water (110°F/43°C)

3½–4 cups (17½–20 oz/545–625 ml)
  unbleached bread flour

1 tablespoon plus ½ cup (4 oz/125 g)
  sugar

2 lb (1 kg) Thompson Red Flame or
  other seedless red grapes

2 tablespoons olive oil, plus extra for
  pans

½ teaspoon salt

*I*n a large bowl or the bowl of an electric stand mixer, dissolve
1 teaspoon of the yeast in 1 cup (8 fl oz/250 ml) of the lukewarm water. Stir in 1 cup (5 oz/155 g) of the flour and the 1
tablespoon sugar. Cover with a kitchen towel and let rise in a
warm place until doubled, 45–60 minutes. (This is known as
the "sponge.")

Meanwhile, stem the grapes, rinse them well and pat dry.
Place in a bowl and toss with the ½ cup (4 oz/125 g) sugar.

In a large bowl, dissolve the remaining 1¼ teaspoons yeast in
the remaining ½ cup (4 fl oz/125 ml) lukewarm water. Stir in the
sponge, the 2 tablespoons olive oil and the salt. Gradually stir
in 2½ cups (12½ oz/390 g) more flour to make a soft dough
that holds its shape.

Knead by hand or with a dough hook, adding flour as necessary. Knead by hand until smooth and elastic, about 10 minutes;
knead by hook until dough is not sticky and pulls cleanly from
the bowl sides, 6–7 minutes. (See directions on pages 10–11.)

Form the dough into a ball and place in a clean, greased
bowl, turning to grease all sides. Cover with plastic wrap and
let rise in a warm place until doubled, 45–60 minutes.

Grease 2 pizza pans, each 12–14 inches (30–35 cm) in
diameter, or 2 baking sheets with olive oil. Turn out the dough
onto a lightly floured work surface and press flat. Cut in half
and form each half into a ball. Dust with flour and let rest for
5 minutes. Using a rolling pin, roll out each half into a round
12–14 inches (30–35 cm) in diameter. Lay the rounds in the
prepared pans and sprinkle evenly with the sugared grapes.
Cover with greased plastic wrap and let rise until doubled,
25–35 minutes. Preheat an oven to 400°F (200°C).

Uncover the rounds and bake until golden brown, about 20
minutes. Cut into pieces and serve warm.

Makes two 1½-lb (750-g) flat breads

Tomato and Cheese Pizza

FOR THE DOUGH:

olive oil

2½–3 cups (12½–15 oz/390–470 g)
unbleached bread flour

1 teaspoon quick-rise yeast

½ teaspoon salt

1 cup (8 fl oz/250 ml) lukewarm water
(110°F/43°C)

FOR THE TOMATO AND CHEESE TOPPING:

6 ripe tomatoes, about 2 lb (1 kg), sliced

2 tablespoons well-drained capers

4 teaspoons chopped fresh oregano or
2 teaspoons dried oregano

1 lb (500 g) mozzarella, Monterey Jack
or Swiss cheese, thinly sliced

2 cans (2 oz/60 g each) anchovies
packed in olive oil, drained and cut
in half lengthwise (optional)

4 teaspoons olive oil

Pizza dough can be made quickly in a food processor.

❧

To make the dough, lightly grease a large mixing bowl with olive oil. In a food processor fitted with the metal blade, combine 2½ cups (12½ oz/390g) of the flour, the yeast and salt. Pulse briefly to combine. With the motor running, pour in the lukewarm water and process until the mixture clings together, about 25 seconds. If it is too wet, add as much of the remaining flour, ¼ cup (¼ oz/37 g) at a time, as needed to form a mass.

Turn out the dough onto a lightly floured work surface and gather it into a loose ball. (The dough will be slightly soft and sticky.) Place it in the greased bowl and turn the dough to grease all sides. Cover with plastic wrap and let rise in a warm place until doubled, 35–45 minutes.

Oil 2 pizza pans or baking sheets. Turn out the dough onto a lightly floured work surface and press flat. Cut in half and form each half into a ball. Dust lightly with flour and let rest for 5 minutes. Using a rolling pin, roll out each ball into a 12-inch (30-cm) round, making the edges a little thicker than the center. Lay each round on a prepared pan, cover lightly with greased plastic wrap and let rise in a warm place until puffy, 15–20 minutes. Preheat an oven to 400°F (200°C).

Uncover the dough rounds and top evenly with the tomato slices. Sprinkle evenly with the capers and oregano. Top evenly with the cheese. If using the anchovies, arrange them in a lattice pattern on each pizza. Sprinkle evenly with the olive oil.

Bake until the crust is golden and crispy around the edges, about 20 minutes. Cut into wedges and serve warm.

Makes two 12-inch (30-cm) pizzas

Swedish Cardamom Twist

3½–4 cups (17½–20 oz/545–625 g)
  unbleached bread flour

¼ teaspoon salt

¼ cup (2 oz/60 g) sugar

1 package (2¼ teaspoons) quick-rise
  yeast

½ cup (4 fl oz/125 ml) milk

¼ cup (2 oz/60 g) unsalted butter

½ cup (4 fl oz/125 ml) water

seeds from 12 cardamom pods, crushed
  (*see glossary, page 104*)

FILLING:

¼ cup (2 oz/60 g) unsalted butter, at
  room temperature, cut into pieces

¼ cup (2 oz/60 g) sugar

¾ teaspoon ground cinnamon

1 egg yolk beaten with 1 teaspoon
  water, for glaze

*I*n a large bowl, combine 1 cup (5 oz/155 g) of the flour, the salt, sugar and yeast and mix well. In a pan over low heat, combine the milk, butter, water and cardamom seeds. Heat to lukewarm (110°F/43°C). Beat the milk mixture into the flour mixture until smooth. Gradually beat in 2½ cups (12½ oz/390 g) more flour to make a soft dough that holds its shape.

Knead by hand or with a dough hook, adding flour as necessary. Knead by hand until smooth and elastic, about 10 minutes; knead by hook until dough is not sticky and pulls cleanly from the bowl sides, 6–7 minutes. (See directions on pages 10–11.)

Form the dough into a ball and place in a clean, greased bowl, turning to grease all sides. Cover with plastic wrap and let rise in a warm place until doubled, 1½–2 hours.

Meanwhile, make the filling: In a small bowl, cream together the butter, sugar and cinnamon.

Turn out the dough onto a floured work surface and press flat. Form into a ball and knead for about 1 minute until smooth and shiny. Cover with a kitchen towel and let rest for 10 minutes. Using a rolling pin, roll out the dough into a 9-by-12-inch (23-by-30-cm) rectangle. Spread the filling evenly over the dough, leaving a 1-inch (2.5-cm) border on all sides. Starting at a long side, roll up the rectangle like a jelly roll and pinch the seam and ends to seal. Flour a baking sheet. Place the roll, seam side down, on the sheet. Snip the dough and pull the sections apart as directed on page 13. Cover with greased plastic wrap and let rise until doubled, about 1 hour.

Preheat an oven to 375°F (190°C). Brush the loaf with the glaze. Bake until golden brown, 25–30 minutes. Transfer to a wire rack to cool.

Makes one 1¾-lb (875-g) loaf

Hot Cross Buns

1¼ cups (10 fl oz/310 ml) lukewarm milk (110°F/43°C)

1 package (2¼ teaspoons) active dry yeast

3½–4 cups (17½–20 oz/545–625 g) unbleached bread flour

1 teaspoon salt

3 tablespoons golden brown sugar

½ teaspoon ground nutmeg

½ teaspoon ground cinnamon

¼ teaspoon ground cloves

¼ teaspoon ground allspice

2 eggs, at room temperature

3 tablespoons unsalted butter, at room temperature, cut into small pieces

½ cup (3 oz/90 g) dried currants

½ cup (3 oz/90 g) golden raisins (sultanas)

¼ cup (2 fl oz/60 ml) milk and ½ cup (2 oz/60 g) sugar heated to bubbling, for glaze

*P*our the lukewarm milk into a small bowl and whisk in the yeast and ½ cup (2½ oz/75 g) of the flour. Let stand until bubbly, about 10 minutes. In a large bowl or the bowl of an electric stand mixer, combine 3 cups (15 oz/470 g) of the flour, the salt, brown sugar, nutmeg, cinnamon, cloves and allspice. Stir in the yeast mixture. Beat in the eggs, one at a time, then beat in the butter.

Knead by hand or with a dough hook, adding flour as necessary. Knead by hand until smooth and elastic, about 10 minutes; knead by hook until dough is not sticky and pulls cleanly from the bowl sides, 6–7 minutes. (See directions on pages 10–11.) The dough will be soft.

Form the dough into a ball and place in a clean, greased bowl, turning to grease all sides. Cover with a kitchen towel and let rise in a warm place until doubled, 1½–2 hours.

Turn out the dough onto a lightly floured work surface and press flat. Scatter the currants and raisins over the dough. Fold in half, then knead to distribute the fruits. Dust lightly with flour and let rest for 10 minutes.

Grease and flour a baking sheet. On the work surface, roll the dough into a log 9 inches (23 cm) long. Cut into 18 equal pieces. Knead each piece into a ball. Arrange the balls, well spaced, on the prepared sheet. Cover with a kitchen towel and let rise until doubled, about 40 minutes. Preheat an oven to 400°F (200°C).

Place a shallow pan of boiling water on the oven floor. Using a sharp knife, slash a cross ½ inch (12 mm) deep on each bun. Bake until golden brown, 15–20 minutes. Transfer the buns to a wire rack and immediately brush with the hot glaze. Serve slightly warm.

Makes 18 buns

Spiced Fruit Loaf

2 cups (10 oz/315 g) brown-rice flour,
 plus extra for dusting
⅔ cup (2½ oz/75 g) cornstarch
 (cornflour)
½ teaspoon salt
3 tablespoons granulated sugar
2 teaspoons xanthan gum powder
1 teaspoon baking soda (bicarbonate
 of soda)
½ teaspoon baking powder
¼ teaspoon ground cloves
¼ teaspoon ground nutmeg
¼ cup (2 oz/60 g) cold unsalted butter,
 cut into pieces
½ cup (3 oz/90 g) dried currants
½ cup (3 oz/90 g) golden raisins
 (sultanas)
grated zest of 1 small orange
1 egg
1 cup (8 oz/250 g) plain lowfat yogurt
confectioners' (icing) sugar

This easy-to-make soda bread is similar to German Christmas stollen. It contains no wheat flour, and is thus an ideal holiday treat for those who cannot tolerate wheat. Both nutty-tasting brown-rice flour and xanthan gum powder (a natural product that adds "stretch" to gluten-free flours) can be found at natural-food stores or in mail-order catalogs specializing in flours and grains.

℮

*P*lace a heavy baking sheet in the oven and preheat to 425°F (220°C).

In a large bowl, mix together the 2 cups (10 oz/315 g) rice flour, cornstarch, salt, sugar, xanthan gum powder, baking soda, baking powder, cloves and nutmeg. Using your fingertips, lightly rub in the butter until the mixture resembles coarse meal. Add the currants, raisins and orange zest and stir to distribute evenly.

In a separate bowl, stir together the egg and yogurt until well blended. Pour the egg mixture into the flour mixture and mix quickly with a rubber spatula. Gather the soft dough together and turn it out onto a work surface lightly dusted with brown-rice flour. Form into a ball, then quickly knead a few times until smooth. Cut in half. Using a rolling pin, roll out each half into a 9-by-7-inch (23-by-18-cm) oval. Fold each oval over as if closing a book, making the top layer slightly narrower, to form a "step." Using a large spatula, transfer the loaves to the preheated baking sheet.

Bake until well risen and golden brown, about 25 minutes. Transfer the loaves to a wire rack to cool. Before serving, dust the tops with confectioners' sugar.

Makes two 18-oz (560-g) loaves

Pandolce Genovese

1 package (2¼ teaspoons) quick-rise
  yeast
1 cup (8 fl oz/250 ml) lukewarm water
  (110°F/43°C)
5½–6 cups (27½–30 oz/860–940 g)
  unbleached bread flour
1 cup (8 fl oz/250 ml) lukewarm milk
  (110°F/43°C)
1½ teaspoons salt
½ cup (4 oz/125 g) unsalted butter,
  melted and cooled to lukewarm
  (110°F/43°C), plus 1 tablespoon
  melted butter for glaze
½ cup (4 oz/125 g) sugar
2 tablespoons orange flower water or
  2 teaspoons grated orange zest
2 teaspoons vanilla extract (essence)
1 teaspoon aniseeds
¼ cup (1 oz/30 g) pine nuts, lightly
  toasted in a dry frying pan
1 cup (6 oz/185 g) golden raisins
  (sultanas), soaked in ¼ cup (2 fl oz/
  60 ml) Marsala for 30 minutes, then
  drained and patted dry
½ cup (3 oz/90 g) candied lemon or
  orange peel, finely chopped (*recipe
  on page 14*)

This Italian sweet bread is popular at year-end festivities.

❧

*I*n the bowl of an electric stand mixer, dissolve 1 teaspoon of the yeast in the lukewarm water. Let stand until bubbles start to rise, about 5 minutes. Add 3 cups (15 oz/470 g) of the flour and stir well. Knead with a dough hook until dough is no longer sticky and pulls cleanly from the bowl sides, about 5 minutes.

Form the dough into a ball and place in a warmed, greased bowl, turning to grease all sides. Cover with plastic wrap and let rise in a warm place until doubled, 50–60 minutes.

Wash and dry the mixer bowl and hook. In the bowl, dissolve the remaining yeast in the milk. Let stand until bubbles start to rise, about 5 minutes. Stir in 2½ cups (12½ oz/390 g) of the flour, the salt, melted butter, sugar, orange water or zest, vanilla and aniseeds. Add the risen dough and knead with the hook, adding flour as needed, until smooth and elastic, about 12 minutes.

Place in a clean, greased bowl, turning the dough to grease all sides. Cover with plastic wrap; let rise until doubled, 1½–2 hours.

Turn out the dough onto a work surface and press flat. Scatter the pine nuts, raisins and candied peel over the top. Roll up like a jelly roll and knead briefly to distribute evenly. Cover with a kitchen towel and let rest for 10 minutes.

Grease and flour two 8-inch (20-cm) round cake pans. Cut the dough in half and form 2 balls, stretching the sides down and under. Place a ball in the center of each pan, cover with greased plastic wrap and let rise until more than doubled and the dough reaches the pan sides, about 1½ hours. Preheat an oven to 375°F (190°C). Using a sharp knife, slash a large triangle on each loaf.

Bake until dark golden brown, 35–40 minutes. Transfer to a rack, glaze the hot loaves with melted butter and let cool.

Makes two 1¾-lb (875-g) loaves

97

Greek Easter Bread

1 bay leaf

¼ teaspoon mahaleb, optional
(*see glossary, page 105*)

½ teaspoon ground cinnamon

½ teaspoon aniseeds

1 teaspoon grated lemon zest

1 cup (8 fl oz/250 ml) water

½ cup (4 fl oz/125 ml) milk

½ cup (4 oz/125 g) unsalted butter

3 eggs, beaten

½ cup (4 oz/125 g) sugar

1 teaspoon salt

1 package (2¼ teaspoons) quick-rise
yeast

6½–7 cups (32–35 oz/1–1.1 kg)
unbleached bread flour

2 eggs, hard-cooked and dyed red

1 egg white beaten with 1 teaspoon
water, for glaze

2 tablespoons sesame seeds

*I*n a small saucepan, combine the bay leaf, mahaleb (if using), cinnamon, aniseeds, lemon zest and ½ cup (4 fl oz/125 ml) of the water. Bring to a boil, remove from the heat and let cool to lukewarm (110°F/43°C). Remove the bay leaf and discard. In a separate saucepan, combine the remaining ½ cup (4 fl oz/125 ml) water, milk and butter and heat to lukewarm (110°F/43°C).

In a large bowl or the bowl of an electric stand mixer, combine the beaten eggs, the milk mixture and spice mixture. Stir in the sugar, salt and yeast. Gradually stir in 5 cups (25 oz/780 g) of the flour to make a soft dough that holds its shape.

Knead by hand or with a dough hook, adding flour as necessary. Knead by hand until smooth and elastic, about 15 minutes; knead by hook until dough is not sticky and pulls cleanly from the bowl sides, 6–7 minutes. (See directions on pages 10–11.)

Form it into a ball and place in a clean, greased bowl, turning to grease all sides. Cover with plastic wrap and let rise in a warm place until doubled, 1½–2 hours.

Turn out the dough onto a lightly floured work surface and press flat. Cut off one-fifth. Cut the larger piece in half and form into 2 rounds each 8 inches (20 cm) in diameter. Cut the small piece into 8 equal pieces and roll each into a rope 12 inches (30 cm) long. Twist pairs of the ropes together. Make an indentation on top of each loaf and place a red egg in it. Crisscross 2 ropes over each egg; secure them under the loaf. Place each loaf on a floured baking sheet, cover with a kitchen towel and let rise until doubled, 60–75 minutes.

Preheat an oven to 350°F (180°C).

Uncover the loaves, brush with the glaze (avoiding the eggs) and sprinkle with the sesame seeds. Bake until golden brown, 40–45 minutes. Transfer the loaves to a wire rack to cool.

Makes two 30-oz (940-g) loaves

Cornish Saffron Bread

¼ teaspoon saffron threads

⅓ cup (3 fl oz/80 ml) boiling water

1 package (2¼ teaspoons) quick-rise yeast

6 tablespoons (3 oz/90 g) unsalted butter

⅔ cup (5 fl oz/160 ml) milk

about 3½ cups (17½ oz/545 g) unbleached bread flour

3 tablespoons sugar

1 teaspoon salt

½ teaspoon ground nutmeg

½ cup (3 oz/90 g) golden raisins (sultanas)

½ cup (3 oz/90 g) dried currants

¼ cup (1½ oz/45 g) chopped candied lemon peel *(recipe on page 14)*

1 egg yolk beaten with 1 teaspoon water, for glaze

This bread of England's West Country is often served with tea.

℮

Crumble the saffron into a small bowl and add the boiling water. Let cool for 15 minutes. Add the yeast and stir to dissolve. In a pan over low heat, combine the butter and milk. Heat until the butter melts, then let cool to lukewarm (110°F/43°C).

In a large bowl or the bowl of an electric stand mixer, combine 2½ cups (12½ oz/390 g) of the flour, the sugar, salt and nutmeg. Stir in the saffron and butter mixtures. Stir in enough of the remaining flour to make a soft dough that holds its shape.

Knead by hand or with a dough hook, adding flour as necessary. Knead by hand until smooth and elastic, about 10 minutes; knead by hook until dough is not sticky and pulls cleanly from the bowl sides, 6–7 minutes. (See directions on pages 10–11.)

Form the dough into a ball and place in a clean, greased bowl, turning to grease all sides. Cover with plastic wrap and let rise in a warm place until doubled, 60–75 minutes.

Grease two 8½-by-4½-inch (21.5-by-11.5-cm) loaf pans. Turn out the dough onto a lightly floured work surface and press flat. Scatter on the raisins, currants and lemon peel, roll up like a jelly roll and knead to distribute the fruits evenly. Cut in half. Using a rolling pin, roll out each half into a 12-by-7-inch (30-by-18-cm) rectangle. Starting at a short side, roll up each rectangle and pinch the seams to seal. Place in the prepared pans, seam sides down. Cover with a kitchen towel and let rise until doubled, about 1 hour. Preheat an oven to 400°F (200°C).

Brush the loaves with the glaze. Bake for 10 minutes, then reduce the heat to 375°F (190°C) and bake until well browned and the loaves sound hollow when tapped on the bottoms, 25–30 minutes longer. Transfer to a wire rack to cool.

Makes two 22-oz (685-g) loaves

Harvest Wheat Sheaf Bread

1 package (2¼ teaspoons) quick-rise yeast

3½–4 cups (17½–20 oz/545–625 g) unbleached bread flour

I cups (8 fl oz/350 ml) lukewarm water (110°F/43°C)

2 teaspoons salt

1 tablespoon vegetable oil

1 egg beaten with 2 teaspoons water, for glaze

Here is a wonderful centerpiece for a Thanksgiving table.

❧

*I*n a large bowl or the bowl of an electric stand mixer, combine the yeast, ½ cup (2½ oz/75 g) of the flour and 1 cup (8 fl oz/ 250 ml) of the lukewarm water. Let stand until bubbly, about 10 minutes. Stir in the salt, oil and 2 cups (10 oz/315 g) more flour until well combined. Gradually stir in another 1 cup (5 oz/155 g) of the flour to make a soft dough that holds its shape.

Knead by hand or with a dough hook, adding flour as necessary. Knead by hand until smooth and elastic, about 10 minutes; knead by hook until dough is not sticky and pulls cleanly from the bowl sides, 6–7 minutes. (See directions on pages 10–11.)

Form the dough into a ball and place in a clean, greased bowl, turning to grease all sides. Cover with plastic wrap and let rise in a warm place until doubled, 60–75 minutes.

Turn out the dough onto a lightly floured work surface and press flat. Divide into thirds and form each portion into a ball. Cover with a kitchen towel and let rest for 10 minutes. Grease and flour a heavy baking sheet.

To make the wheat sheaf base, roll out 1 ball of dough into an oval 12 inches (30 cm) long and 9 inches (23 cm) wide. Cut away a small rectangle 2 by 3 inches (5 by 7.5 cm) from opposite sides on one end of the oval, forming a tall mushroom shape. Transfer to the prepared baking sheet. Decorate the wheat sheaf following the directions on page 13. Cover with a kitchen towel and let rise until puffy, about 30 minutes. Preheat an oven to 400°F (200°C).

Brush the loaf with the remaining egg glaze. Bake until well risen and golden brown, 40–45 minutes. Transfer to a wire rack to cool.

Makes one 22-oz (685-g) loaf

Glossary

The following glossary defines terms specifically as they relate to bread making, including major and unusual ingredients.

ALLSPICE
Sweet spice of Caribbean origin with a flavor suggesting a blend of **cinnamon, cloves** and **nutmeg,** hence its name. May be purchased as whole dried berries or ground.

ANCHOVIES
Tiny saltwater fish, related to sardines, most commonly found as canned fillets that have been salted and preserved in oil. Imported anchovy fillets packed in olive oil are the most commonly available; anchovies packed in salt, available canned in some Italian delicatessens, are considered the finest. Rinse salt-packed anchovies before using.

BAKING POWDER
Commercial baking product combining three ingredients: **baking soda** (bicarbonate of soda), the source of the carbon-dioxide gas that causes quick bread batters and dough to rise; an acid, such as cream of tartar, calcium acid phosphate or sodium aluminum sulphate, which, when the powder is combined with a liquid, causes the baking soda to release its gas; and a starch such as cornstarch or flour, to keep the powder from absorbing moisture.

BAKING SODA
Also known as bicarbonate of soda or sodium bicarbonate, the active component of **baking powder** and the source of the carbon dioxide gas that leavens quick bread batters and doughs. Often used on its own to leaven batters that include acidic ingredients such as **buttermilk, yogurt** or citrus juices.

BUTTER
For bread-making purposes, unsalted butter is preferred. To soften butter, let it stand at room temperature for at least 30 minutes before use. Or place it unwrapped on a microwaveproof plate or in a bowl, or wrap in waxed paper or plastic wrap, and put it in a microwave oven; with the oven set on high, heat the butter for 20 seconds, stopping to check its consistency and repeating as necessary until it is soft enough to mash easily with a fork.

BUTTERMILK
Form of cultured low-fat or nonfat milk that contributes a tangy flavor and thick, creamy texture to breads, particularly those leavened with **baking soda** (bicarbonate of soda). Its acidity also provides a boost to leavening agents.

CAPERS
Small, pickled buds of a bush common to the Mediterranean, used as a savory flavoring or garnish.

CARDAMOM
Sweet, exotic-tasting spice, mainly used in Middle Eastern and Indian cooking and in European baking. Its small, round seeds, which grow enclosed inside a husklike pod, are best purchased whole, then ground with a spice grinder or with a mortar and pestle as needed.

CINNAMON
Popular sweet spice for flavoring baked goods. The aromatic bark of a type of evergreen tree, it is sold as whole dried strips—cinnamon sticks—or ground.

CARDAMOM

CLOVES
Rich and aromatic East African spice used whole or in its ground form to flavor both sweet and savory recipes.

COCOA, UNSWEETENED
Richly flavored, fine-textured powder ground from the solids left after much of the cocoa butter has been extracted from chocolate liquor. Cocoa powder specially treated to reduce its natural acidity, resulting in a darker color and more mellow flavor, is known as Dutch-process cocoa.

CORN SYRUP
Neutral-tasting syrup extracted from corn. Sold either as unfiltered dark corn syrup or filtered light corn syrup.

CHEESES
Whether incorporated into doughs or batters or used as a topping, cheese adds richness and flavor to all kinds of breads.

Monterey Jack
Semisoft, creamy white melting cheese with a mild flavor and buttery texture.

Mozzarella
Rindless white, mild-tasting Italian cheese traditionally made from water buffalo's milk and sold fresh. Commercially produced and packaged cow's milk mozzarella is now far more common, although it has less flavor.

Swiss Cheese
Firm whole-milk cheese, pale creamy yellow in color, with distinctive holes that grow larger and more numerous with ripening. Popular, on its own or in recipes, for its mild, slightly sweet, nutlike flavor.

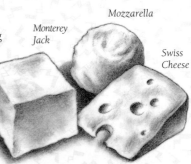

Mozzarella

Monterey Jack

Swiss Cheese

CORNSTARCH

Also known as cornflour, this fine, powdery flour is ground from the endosperm of corn (the white heart of the kernel). Because it contains no gluten, it is used to give a delicate texture to baked goods. Also, when mixed with water, it makes a transparent glaze for brushing on loaves before baking.

CURRANTS, DRIED

Produced from a variety of small grapes, these dried fruits resemble tiny **raisins** but have a stronger, tarter flavor. Sold in the baking section of food stores. If unavailable, substitute raisins.

EGGS

Although eggs are sold in the United States in a range of sizes, large grade A eggs are the most common size and should be used for the recipes in this book.

To separate an egg, crack the shell in half by tapping it against the side of a bowl and then breaking it apart with your fingers. Holding the shell halves over the bowl (below), gently transfer the whole yolk back and forth between them, letting the clear white drop away into the bowl. Transfer the yolk to another bowl.

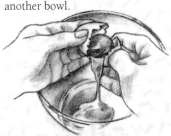

Alternatively, gently pour the egg from the shell onto the slightly cupped fingers of your clean, outstretched hand held over a bowl. Let the whites fall between your fingers into the bowl; the whole yolk will remain in your hand.

The same basic function is also performed by an aluminum, ceramic or plastic egg separator placed over a bowl. The separator holds the yolk intact in its cuplike center while allowing the white to drip out through one or more slots in its side into the bowl.

GARLIC

Pungent bulb popular worldwide as a flavoring ingredient, both raw and cooked. For the best flavor, purchase whole heads of dry garlic, separating individual cloves from the head as needed; it is best not to purchase more than you will use in 1 or 2 weeks, as garlic can shrivel and lose its flavor with prolonged storage.

To peel a garlic clove, place on a work surface and cover with the side of a large chef's knife. Press down firmly on the side of the knife to crush the clove slightly; the dry skin will then slip off easily.

GRAPES, THOMPSON RED FLAME

Popular American variety of medium-sized, sweet, red-skinned seedless grapes. Other red seedless grapes may be substituted.

HERBES DE PROVENCE

A commercially sold dried herb blend typical of the Provence region of south-central France. It may include **oregano,** thyme, savory and such other local seasonings as marjoram, **rosemary,** basil and lavender blossoms.

HONEY

The natural, sweet, syruplike substance produced by bees from flower nectar, honey is popular both as a sweetener for bread doughs and batters and as a spread for baked bread. In its color, taste and aroma, it subtly reflects the blossoms from which it was made.

Honeys from clover and orange blossoms are light in color and flavor. Heather honey has a deeper, red-brown color and richer taste. Honeys derived from herb blossoms, such as thyme, have similarly distinctive aromatic tastes.

MAHALEB

Small, pale brown seed—slightly smaller than a coriander seed—that is the kernel of a black cherry stone. An especially popular flavoring in the cooking of Syria. Look for the whole spice in Middle Eastern markets. Pulverize in a mortar with a pestle or grind in a spice grinder before using.

MARSALA

Dry or sweet amber Italian wine from the area of Marsala, on the island of Sicily.

MOLASSES

Thick, robust-tasting, syrupy sugarcane by-product of sugar refining, a procedure that may or may not include the use of sulfur. Light molasses results from the first boiling of the syrup; dark molasses from the second boiling. Either type of molasses can be used in most bread recipes with darker varieties of molasses yielding a more intense flavor than lighter ones.

NUTMEG

Popular baking spice that is the hard pit of the fruit of the nutmeg tree. May be bought already ground or, for fresher flavor, whole to be grated as needed. Whole nutmegs may be kept inside special nutmeg graters, which include hinged flaps that conceal a storage compartment. Freshly grate nutmeg as needed, steadying one end of a grater on a work surface (below). Return unused portion of whole nutmeg to compartment.

OILS

Oils may be used in bread doughs to enrich or flavor them or to serve as a shortening agent. When the term "vegetable oil" is used, it refers to any of several refined pure or blended oils pressed or otherwise extracted from any of a number of sources—including corn, cottonseed, peanuts, safflower seeds, soybeans and sunflower seeds—which are prized for their pale color and neutral flavor. A wide variety of olive oils are available in most markets. Each brand varies both in color (from golden to deep green) and in flavor (from fruity to herbaceous); choose one that suits your taste. The higher-priced extra-virgin olive oils, made from the first pressing of the olives, are usually of better quality; products labeled pure olive oil are less aromatic and flavorful. Walnut oil, popular in dressings and as a seasoning, conveys the rich taste of the nuts from which it is pressed; seek out oil made from lightly toasted nuts, which has a full but not too assertive flavor.

NUTS
Rich and mellow in flavor, crisp and crunchy in texture, a wide variety of nuts may be included in or atop bread doughs and batters. For the best selection, look in a specialty-food shop, health-food store or the baking section of a food store. Some of the most popular options include:

Pecans
Brown-skinned, crinkly textured nuts with a distinctive sweet, rich flavor and crisp, slightly crumbly texture. Native to the southern United States.

Pine Nuts
Small, ivory seeds extracted from the cones of a species of pine tree, with a rich, slightly resinous flavor.

Walnuts
Rich, crisp-textured nuts with distinctively crinkled surfaces. English walnuts, the most familiar variety, are grown worldwide, although the largest crops are in California.

To Chop Nuts
Spread the nuts in a single layer on a nonslip cutting surface. Using a chef's knife, chop the nuts by holding the tip of the knife blade steady against the cutting surface and bringing the handle of the knife up and down over the nuts.

Alternatively, put a handful or two of nuts in a food processor fitted with the metal blade and use a few rapid on-off pulses to chop the nuts to desired consistency; repeat with the remaining nuts in batches. Be careful not to process the nuts too long or their oils will be released and the nuts will turn into a paste.

OLIVES, OIL-CURED BLACK
Throughout Mediterranean Europe, ripe black olives are cured in combinations of salt, seasonings, brines, vinegars and oils to produce pungently flavored results. Good-quality oil-cured olives are available in delicatessens and well-stocked food stores.

ONION, YELLOW
Common, white-fleshed, strong-flavored onion distinguished by its dry, yellowish brown skin.

ORANGE FLOWER WATER
A sweet, aromatic essence distilled from the natural oils present in orange petals and used as a subtle flavoring in Middle Eastern and other cuisines. Available in the liquor department of most markets and in liquor stores.

OREGANO
Aromatic, pungent and spicy Mediterranean herb—also known as wild marjoram—used fresh or dried as a seasoning in savory dishes and some Italian breads.

PANCETTA
Italian-style unsmoked bacon cured with salt and pepper. May be sold flat like regular bacon slices or rolled into a large sausage shape to be sliced as needed (below). Available in Italian delicatessens and specialty-food stores.

POTATOES, BAKING
Large potatoes with thick brown skins and a dry, mealy texture when cooked. They contribute fine, dense texture and earthy flavor to potato breads. Also known as russet or Idaho potatoes.

RAISINS
Variety of dried grapes, popular as a snack on their own. For baking, use seedless dark raisins or golden raisins (sultanas).

ROSEMARY
Mediterranean herb, used either fresh or dried, with an intense, aromatic flavor that calls for sparing use.

SAFFRON
Intensely aromatic spice, golden orange in color, made from the dried stigmas of a species of crocus. Imparts a delicate perfume and golden hue to baked goods, especially those of Mediterranean origin. Sold either as threads—the dried stigmas—or in powdered form. Look for products labeled pure saffron.

SALT
A little common table salt is added to most bread doughs to enhance their flavor. Larger grains of salt may be used as a topping for loaves or rolls. Coarse salt, about the size of tiny pebbles, is similar in composition and taste to table salt. Kosher salt is a smaller flaked coarse-grained salt with no additives and a less salty taste than table salt. Salt extracted by evaporation from sea water is known as sea salt. It has a more pronounced flavor than regular table salt and is available in both coarse and fine grinds.

STOUT

Variety of beer, originating in the British Isles, which derives its distinctively rich, bitter flavor and dark brown color from a high proportion of hops and the addition of roasted barley. Guinness, from Ireland, is the best-known and one of the most popular brands.

SUGARS

Several different forms of sugar may be used in breads. Brown sugar is a rich combination of granulated sugar and **molasses** in varying quantities; available as golden, light or dark brown sugar, with crystals varying from coarse to finely granulated. Confectioners' sugar is finely pulverized sugar, also known as powdered or icing sugar, which dissolves quickly to produce a thin, white decorative coating for sweet breads and cakes. To prevent confectioners' sugar from absorbing moisture in the air and caking, manufacturers often mix a little **cornstarch** into it. Granulated sugar is the standard, widely used form of pure white sugar. Do not use superfine granulated sugar unless specified in recipes.

TOMATOES

During the summer months, when tomatoes are in season, use the best red or yellow sun-ripened tomatoes you can find. At other times of year, plum tomatoes, sometimes called Roma or egg tomatoes, are likely to have the best flavor and texture.

VANILLA EXTRACT

Flavoring derived by dissolving the essential oil of the vanilla bean in an alcohol base. Use only products labeled pure or natural vanilla extract (essence).

VINEGAR

Literally "sour wine," vinegar results when certain strains of yeast cause wine—or some other alcoholic liquid such as apple cider or Japanese rice wine—to ferment for a second time, turning it acidic. The best-quality wine vinegars begin with good-quality wine. Red wine vinegar, like the wine from which it is made, has a more robust flavor than vinegar produced from white wine.

XANTHAN GUM POWDER

A natural carbohydrate derivative of corn syrup, this powdery substance is used in breads made from gluten-free flours, to add springiness to the dough.

YEAST

Active dry yeast, one of the most widely available forms of yeast for baking, is commonly sold in individual packages containing about 2¼ teaspoons and found in the baking section of food stores. Also popular with many bakers is quick-rise yeast, which raises bread doughs in about half the time of regular active dry yeast. If using fresh cake yeast, substitute ½ oz (15 g) for 1 package active dry yeast.

YOGURT, PLAIN LOW-FAT

Yogurt is made from milk that is fermented by bacterial cultures. It imparts a mildly acidic flavor to breads and adds a boost to leaveners such as **baking soda** (bicarbonate of soda). So-called plain yogurt simply refers to the unflavored product, to distinguish it from the many popular varieties of flavored and sweetened yogurt. Available made from whole, low-fat or nonfat milk.

ZEST

Thin, brightly colored, outermost layer of a citrus fruit's peel, containing most of its aromatic essential oils—a lively source of flavor for breads. Zest may be removed using one of two easy methods: Use a simple tool known as a zester, drawing its sharp-edged holes across the fruit's skin to remove the zest in thin strips (below).

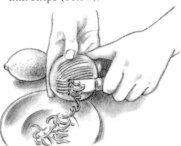

Alternatively, use the fine holes on a hand-held grater or shredder.

Or, holding the edge of a paring knife or vegetable peeler (below) away from you and almost parallel to the fruit's skin, carefully cut off the zest in thin strips, taking care not to remove any of the bitter white pith with it. Then thinly slice or chop the strips on a cutting board.

SEEDS

A variety of tiny seeds offer flavor and rustic texture to breads. They can be used both as a topping and an ingredient in bread doughs. Some of the seeds used in this book include:

Aniseeds

Sweet licorice-flavored spice of Mediterranean origin, the small crescent-shaped seeds (below) of a plant related to parsley. Generally sold as whole seeds, which may be crushed with a mortar and pestle or in a spice grinder.

Caraway Seeds

Small, crescent-shaped dried seeds used whole or ground as a savory seasoning. Caraway seeds are traditionally added to rye bread to provide its distinctive flavor.

Fennel Seeds

Small, crescent-shaped seeds (below) of a plant related to the bulb vegetable of the same name, prized as a spice for their mild anise flavor. Can be used both whole or ground.

Poppy Seeds

Small, spherical, blue-black seeds of a form of poppy; traditionally used in central and eastern European cooking to add rich, nutlike flavor to baked goods.

Sesame Seeds

Tiny, pale ivory-colored seeds with a mild, nutty flavor. Often sprinkled over bread doughs as a topping.

Index

ACKNOWLEDGMENTS

The publishers would like to thank the following people and organizations
for their generous assistance and support in producing this book:
Sharon C. Lott, Stephen W. Griswold, Ken DellaPenta, Sarah Lemas, Tina Schmitz,
Marguerite Ozburn, the buyers and store managers for Pottery Barn and Williams-Sonoma stores.

The following kindly lent props for the photography: Biordi Art Imports,
Candelier, Fillamento, Forrest Jones, Sue Fisher King, RH Shop and Chuck Williams.